The Volunteer Church is an immensely practical and hands-on guide to encouraging, recruiting, motivating, and caring for the volunteers who make our church ministry possible. It is an invaluable tool in helping the members of our churches discover and fulfill their God-given mission.

—Rev. Paul Jorgensen, Cornerstone
Church, Litchfield, MN

The Volunteer Church is a must read for every ministerial and lay leader in the church. I only wish I had had this book early on in my ministry.

—Dr. George O. Wood, General
Superintendent, the General Council of
the Assemblies of God, Springfield, MO

I met two pastors within the last week who lamented their lack of volunteers. Both wondered what God could do if they had more well-trained volunteers to accomplish their mission. And both weren't sure how to solve this problem. They needed this book. You need this book. Read it and discover how to create a culture of volunteering at your church.

—Jason Strand, Teaching Pastor, Eagle
Brook Church, Minneapolis, MN

This is a *now* needed book. *The Volunteer Church* captures the imagination of what church should and could be now and in the future. People are longing to volunteer but need a pathway. Here it is! The weaving of the biblical and historical stories of volunteerism with contemporary examples is a compelling call to action. This is a watershed book for our time, coupled with specific guidance on how to lead a much needed volunteer movement of the kingdom of God on earth. Should be in the hands of every Christian leader!

—Jo Anne Lyon, General Superintendent,
the Wesleyan Church, Fishers, IN

The New Testament paints a vision of the church where every member is equipped for the work of ministry. Ministry is not just for a few paid professionals. Ministry is for every Christ-follower, and this means that ministry is for volunteers. In *The Volunteer Church*, Leith Anderson and Jill Fox provide us with the theological foundation for developing a volunteer culture and the practical advice needed to effectively recruit, train, and care for volunteers. This book should be required reading for all desiring to develop and maintain a volunteer culture in the local church setting.

—Justin A. Irving, PhD,
Professor of Ministry Leadership,
Bethel Seminary, St. Paul, MN

As a pastor, I've grown to appreciate the value of volunteers and the role they play in the life of a church. In *The Volunteer Church*, authors Leith Anderson and Jill Fox discuss the culture of volunteerism and give practical tools for volunteer recruitment and development. This book is a welcome resource for anyone serving in church leadership.

—John K. Jenkins Sr., Senior Pastor,
First Baptist Church of Glenarden,
Upper Marlboro, MD

THE VOLUNTEER CHURCH

MOBILIZING YOUR
CONGREGATION FOR GROWTH
AND EFFECTIVENESS

LEITH ANDERSON & JILL FOX

 ZONDERVAN®

ZONDERVAN

The Volunteer Church
Copyright © 2015 by Leith Anderson and Jill Fox

This title is also available as a Zondervan ebook. Visit www.zondervan.com/ebooks.

Requests for information should be addressed to:

Zondervan, 3900 Sparks Dr. SE, Grand Rapids, Michigan 49546

Library of Congress Cataloging-in-Publication Data

Anderson, Leith, 1944-
    The volunteer church : mobilizing your congregation for growth and effectiveness /
Leith Anderson and Jill Fox.
      pages cm
    Includes bibliographical references.
    ISBN 978-0-310-51915-7 (softcover)
    1. Church personnel management. 2. Lay ministry. 3. Laity. I. Fox, Jill, 1979- II. Title
BV652.13.A53 2015
  253 — dc23   2015002786

Cover design: Brand Navigation
Cover photography: iStockphoto
Interior design: Denise Froehlich

Printed in the United States of America

15 16 17 18 19 20 21 22 23 /DCI/ 20 19 18 17 16 15 14 13 12 11 10 9 8 7 6 5 4 3 2 1

Contents

131442

Introduction

The church. A place where the lost are found, the tired are renewed, the lonely find community, and the brokenhearted are healed. The place where the family of God worships together. The church changes lives, and those changed lives change the world. The heart of the church—large, small, or medium—is its people.

Especially those known as volunteers.

Working with volunteers can be a rewarding and exciting experience—for them as well as for those who recruit, train, and maintain their services. However, if we are honest, we know there are times it can be frustrating. But we also know that volunteers are essential, even vital, to creating growth and new ministries. They are the key to introducing youth and children—and adults too—to Jesus Christ. They have the welcoming smiles at the door, and they serve the food, pray for needs, teach Bible classes, mentor others, stuff bulletins, organize missions trips, and on and on. If you want to see your church grow, it *must* be a volunteering church, a church that *functions* on volunteers.

If you lead a church or parts of its ministry outreach and are exhausted by the lack of volunteer help, this book is for you. If you are a volunteer and dream of adding numbers to your team, this book is for you. If you are on a church staff and know that a new ministry is needed, but volunteers and training are required to make it happen, this book is for you.

So join us on the journey to build the volunteering church.

- Learn how to effectively *recruit and train* volunteers.
- Discover how to *build sustainable, long-lasting ministries* led by volunteers.
- Find methods for *encouraging and maintaining* your volunteers.
- Know how to *build teams* of volunteers.
- Understand how to *find the right service* that fits a willing volunteer.

Whether you are delighted with your volunteers, flustered at the lack, or simply want to improve on what your church is already doing, we invite you to become the volunteering church. You'll see your teams of workers be fulfilled, ministries grow, and the church staff excel.

Part 1

BUILDING A VOLUNTEER CULTURE

1

~~~~~~~~~~~~~~~

People Want to Volunteer

LEITH

Google the phrase "why people volunteer" and about seventy-three million websites and articles will appear. If you read any of them, you'll quickly conclude that people *want* to volunteer. That's good news! And even better, you'll be pleased to learn that religious volunteering tops most of the lists. (Well, some of the lists. I confess I did not have enough time to read all seventy-three million sites.)

Instead of researching on a computer the motivation behind volunteering, though, try looking for the answer in the Bible. You'll find lots of volunteers. You'll find them in the Old Testament book of Judges — individuals who stepped up and answered God's call during some of the troubled times in Israel's history. For example, God raised up an amazing leader named Deborah, who was a prophetess, judge, politician, and military strategist. She was also a songwriter and singer; here's some of her song:

> When the princes in Israel take the lead,
>> when the people willingly offer themselves —
>> praise the LORD!
>
> —JUDGES 5:2

> My heart is with Israel's princes,
>> with the willing volunteers among the people.
>> Praise the LORD!
>
> —JUDGES 5:9

When Deborah sang this, the nation was a real mess—roads were closed, village life had ceased, and there were no arms for an army. So Deborah tapped into a reservoir of waiting volunteers, defeated the occupying enemy, and brought forty years of peace and prosperity to Israel.

Turn your Bible a few pages to the New Testament and you'll find more stories of volunteers in the book of Acts. Willing volunteers in the early church sold their property and shared the proceeds with needy Christians (Acts 4:32–37). When the Jerusalem church got bogged down in a controversy about distributing the benevolence money, a group of financial volunteers stepped up and solved the problem (Acts 6:1–7).

There are many reasons why people volunteer, and we shouldn't assume that we know those reasons. I recall talking to someone on a church-sponsored Mediterranean tour of Israel and Turkey, and I asked this person why he was one of the first people to sign up for the trip. My assumption was that he really wanted to visit the lands of the Bible. But he had an unexpected answer for me: "Honestly, I would have signed up if this was a trip to Florida or Montana. The destination didn't matter. I'm new in town and to the church, and I figured this was a good way to make some friends."

Some people volunteer out of generosity, out of gratitude for God's blessings. Others volunteer out of selfishness, motivated by guilt, shame, or a sense of obligation. Some don't really think about why they volunteer; they just do it. I believe it is helpful to think about our motivations, to understand some of the top reasons why people volunteer. And it's also a good idea to ask your volunteers that question, to learn what they want out of the experience.

Personal Desires

Our personal needs and desires are powerful motivators. Whenever Jesus connected with people, he usually began by speaking to their desires. What do you want? Hungry people wanted food. Blind, leprous, and lame people wanted healing. Curious people wanted to learn, to hear Jesus tell stories. The theologians and religious leaders wanted answers to their questions. Just about everyone wanted to see miracles. Jesus knew that the people around him had needs, including eternal needs that extended beyond their wants. But often, he began by addressing their desires.

Today, there are "seekers" who may come to church looking for a friend. They may not be interested, at first, in a personal relationship with Jesus Christ. So we get to know them. We learn what they are looking for and start with their desires. Maybe we can learn something from Paul on Mars Hill in Athens (Acts 17), where he started his presentation quoting familiar pagan poets rather than Old Testament prophets, and moved on from there to Jesus and the resurrection. God created us as social beings in the image of God, so of course we need friends and meaningful relationships with others. Aloneness can be devastating— just look at the psychological and physical consequences of solitary confinement. God designed us to be together, not all by ourselves. And that's why many people offer to volunteer. They are lonely. They want to be connected. They want friends.

Some will say that this is especially true for men. In many cultures, women socialize around conversation while men socialize around tasks. When lonely men are offered a circle of talk, they may decline; when lonely men are offered a circle of activity, they are likely to accept. When men are invited to volunteer for a sports team, construction project, planning task force, or camping trip, they may agree to the task without admitting they are really looking for friends.

Other people are looking for excitement. Boredom comes in many guises. You may find teenagers who want to volunteer because they couldn't get summer jobs, or you'll find the octogenarian who used to be a world-traveling hostage negotiator and simply wants to stay active. Volunteering is something they want to do rather than staying home and watching television. Others may wish to serve because of job-related boredom. This person may have a very busy life, putting in long hours at the office, factory, or in the driver's seat of an eighteen-wheeler. Though life is full, it's full of the predictable and routine. Volunteering to do relief work in Haiti or to greet newcomers at church services brings some variety and excitement to their lives.

The best physicians don't begin with a prescription; they begin with questions and a diagnosis. Similarly, the best recruiters don't begin with a job offer; they begin by learning about the needs of the volunteer. Don't start with the *church's need* when you ask for help. Begin by saying, "Tell me more about you." Potential volunteers are delighted to be asked, and some will tell you their life story and maybe request a specific service opportunity. Others will leave it to the recruiter to diagnose their need and propose a prescription.

Lofty Aspirations

The eight-year-old boy who approached me between Sunday morning services was smart, though he was the youngest in his third-grade class. He rushed to me and said with excitement in his voice, "I want to be a pastor who wins the whole world to Jesus! What should I do?" I could have explained that he should finish third grade and continue his education through elementary school, middle school, high school, college, seminary, internship, and ordination for the next twenty years. Instead, my advice to this young boy was simple and immediately relevant. "Start with the Bible. Read what it has to say. Learn what it means. That's the best preparation for everything God is calling you to do."

A month later, we had a follow-up conversation in that same hallway between Sunday services. "Okay, I read the entire Bible and figured out everything it says," he told me. "Now I want to know what to do next."

Some volunteers have lofty aspirations.

If you are like most church leaders, when you hear an "over the top" volunteer describing their dream of changing the world, you might want to put the brakes on for them. Over time, leaders develop an intuition that warns them when someone is getting out of control. But I'd caution against trying to dampen this enthusiasm right away. Most volunteers are not delusional or dreaming when they express their desire to do good. They truly want their lives to count, and they wish to make a positive difference in others' lives. Ask questions to make a diagnosis before writing a prescription.

Two of the best Christian volunteers in history were a husband and wife named Priscilla and Aquila. They were lay members of the first-century church of Ephesus. When an amazing Jewish preacher named Apollos of Alexandria visited their church, he mesmerized the congregation with his teaching. According to historian Luke, "He was a learned man, with a thorough knowledge of the Scriptures. He had been instructed in the way of the Lord, and he spoke with great fervor" (Acts 18:24–25).

But there was a problem with this amazing preacher. He "taught about Jesus accurately, though he knew only the baptism of John" (v. 25). He was mostly orthodox with a little bit of baptismal heresy.

Fortunately, Priscilla and Aquila were volunteers in the Ephesian church. They knew their theology, and they wanted to help Apollos. So "when Priscilla and Aquila heard him, they invited him to their home and explained to him the way of God more adequately" (v. 26). They were simply motivated by a desire to help. An interesting footnote to all of this is a claim some New Testament scholars make that Apollos was the author of the New Testament book of Hebrews, counted among the best-written books in the Bible.

Other volunteers serve so they can "make a difference." They are troubled by the pain and poverty in our world, and they know they can't fix everything, but they also believe they can help some. They want to rescue that one girl from sex trafficking, teach that one boy how to read, help that one addict to stay sober, win that one sinner to become a saint, provide that one homeless family with a house, or mentor that one child from a broken home. These people are not looking for recognition, long-term friendship, or a promotion in the social order. They just want to make a difference in someone's life.

You will also find some volunteers who are "legacy" volunteers. They want to start something that will continue when they are gone. They are social and spiritual investors and often have entrepreneurial instincts and gifts. They are far less excited about sustaining existing programs and institutions, but they will light up at the idea of beginning a new church, founding a volunteer network, creating a new Bible study app for mobile phones, constructing new access facilities for the disabled, or inventing a new ministry that none of us would ever have imagined. If you try recruiting them to replace a retiring board member or fill a leadership role, they will likely say no. But they aren't saying no to volunteering; they are saying no because you asked them the wrong question.

Family volunteers are also increasingly popular. In these situations, an entire family signs up to serve together. The initiative to volunteer may come from the parents or the children, but the goals are usually the same. They want to bond as a family while doing something to help others. Often these are families who are grateful for God's blessings and want to "pay it forward" to other families. But don't limit this to the rich helping the poor. Volunteering as a family is a great experience for any family, regardless of their socioeconomic background. Families who have less may not be able to give money or material resources, but they still want to be generous through donating their time and skill. Be aware, however, that when you set up a program for families, you may get more volunteers than you can easily handle. So choose the activities wisely. The benefits far outweigh the risks. Programs designed for multiple families not only allow families to bond with other family members; they also allow the families to bond with other families. This builds community and deepens relationships within your church family.

Finally, some people will volunteer when they are chosen. These are typically Christians with special abilities who are drafted by the church to tackle a difficult assignment, often something they would rather *not* do. These individuals have a high level of trust in God and a deep confidence in the leadership of the church, and so they agree to do what needs to be done, even when it is difficult. An example of this is found in Acts 15. The home church of Christianity in Jerusalem was deeply divided over a controversial theological issue, and it looked like the church was going to split into two denominations, one Jewish and one Gentile. "Then the apostles and elders, with the whole church, decided to choose some of their own men and send them to Antioch with Paul and Barnabas. They chose Judas (called Barsabbas) and Silas, two men who were leaders among the brothers" (Acts 15:22). Judas and Barsabbas agreed to volunteer when asked, and they became instruments used by God to save the young church from schism. They were volunteers who responded to a specific call, sensing they had been chosen by God and had to say yes.

People volunteer for many reasons, but one of the simplest is that they enjoy it. In addition to connecting them to others, volunteering can be fun, even as it brings a sense of fulfillment to their lives. When researchers at the London School of Economics examined the relationship between volunteering and the measures of happiness in a large group of American adults, they found that the more people volunteered, the happier they were. Compared with people who never volunteered, the odds of being "very happy" rose 7 percent among those who volunteered monthly and 12 percent among people who volunteered every two to four weeks. Among weekly

I've often wrestled with two misconceptions about volunteering, and they often rob me of the joy and freedom of serving others.

First, it's too easy to think that with enough love and hard work, I can change the world. Therefore I should say yes to everything I'm asked to do. And when the world doesn't change overnight or even over weeks, my exhausted body and spirit become discouraged, and I wonder what I am doing wrong, what else I need to be doing.

Second, I'm not equipped to do what is being asked of me, so I will not even try. Or I might quit when I've tried something and it has become too difficult. I probably was asked only because they needed somebody to fill the role, not because it's something I'm good at or at which I will succeed.

These delusions stem from looking inward—relying on my strength and skills, focusing on my weaknesses, harnessing my willpower, being paralyzed by my inabilities. Volunteering isn't about what I can do for God; it is accomplishing something with God.

The truth is we are called to do good works, and God will equip us to do those good works. He wants to do them with us and display his power through our lives.

—MICHELLE

volunteers, 16 percent felt very happy—a hike in happiness researchers said was comparable to having an income of $75,000–$100,000 versus $20,000. And among all the volunteer options they surveyed, giving time to religious organizations had the greatest impact.[1]

Today, the competition for volunteers is fierce. Books, websites, and pamphlets are available to guide potential volunteers in finding the right match for their gifts and interests. In an earlier generation, churches may have had a monopoly on the volunteer business, but that is no longer reality. There are limitless opportunities today, and this means that churches must learn how to compete for the time of their own parishioners. There are some churches whose members volunteer thousands of hours a week in their communities, while the congregation is left shorthanded. Extensive opportunities and choices mean that churches must make sure their parishioners are regularly updated on places to volunteer their time and energy in the church. Many of them would be happy to do both community and ministry volunteering.

What about Those Who Say No?

When you ask people to volunteer, prepare to hear some creative reasons why they cannot help. And give people who say no the courtesy of taking them at their word. Usually they are not lying to you, even if they aren't telling you the primary reason why they are declining. We all have our own private catalog of *truthful*, ready-made, polite reasons to decline.

Have you ever had a salesperson stop you in a store, an auto dealership, or an airport and ask, "Is there any reason why you can't sign up for this amazing offer today?" You've probably given one of the usual answers: "I'll have to check with my wife." "I'm a little short on cash right now." "I promised my mother I'd drive her old car at least a hundred thousand miles before trading it in." "I might be transferred to Saudi Arabia, and women can't drive in Saudi Arabia." Seasoned salespersons have good answers for every objection. They also know that objections can be code for saying, "I don't like your cars, and I would never want one even if you gave it to me." Smart code-readers know when to quit. On the other hand, sometimes an excuse is just an excuse. Sometimes a person, with a bit more engagement and questioning, will actually be interested in what you have to offer them—an opportunity to serve.

Consider some of the typical reasons why potential volunteers say no:

1. They don't trust the leaders or the organization.

2. They are scared of the assignment and fearful of failure.

3. They feel taken advantage of because the recruiter isn't really interested in her or him but just wants to fill a vacancy.

4. There is no clear way to get out. If the volunteer position isn't right, doesn't work, or goes terribly wrong, there is no honorable way to quit.

5. The length of commitment is too long. If the potential volunteer is new or has doubts, they're reluctant to commit to every Sunday for a year or more.

6. They are already too busy. Commitments at home and work are overwhelming, and making another commitment risks putting them at the breaking point.

7. They can't say what it is. There is a personal reason, but it is too private to disclose—changing jobs and moving to another city; preg-

nancy; struggling with stress; dysfunctional relationship; cancer diagnosis; financial hardships; problems at home, school, church, or on the job; already looking for a different church to attend.

8. They simply are not interested. They are being asked to do something they can't do or don't want to do.

Let's compare recruiting volunteers to making a marriage proposal. You don't ask someone to marry you unless you know the person already and are fairly confident the answer will be yes. The principle here is that you focus on the person rather than the position. This doesn't mean investing months or years into weekly meetings. It can be as simple as spending an hour of conversation at Starbucks or McDonald's. It's a matter of asking questions, listening, and learning more about who the person is and what the person wants and is gifted to do. If an hour is not enough time, skip the recruiting question at that first meeting and meet again for another hour.

As you get to know your potential volunteers better, you will probably learn some details and can make a good guess at why they decline your offer, so you may want to prepare a possible solution. For example, if you sense that volunteers are going to give you excuse number two—the fear of failure—you can find out more about why they are scared and ask if they would be open to coming to one Sunday school class or one music rehearsal or one basketball game just to watch and listen. Let them test out the opportunity without making a commitment. Suggest that they take some time to think about it, and then email them with a specific time and place to check it out. Tell them that if they are still unsure or uncomfortable, they can reply, "Thanks, but I think I'll decline," and you won't approach them about it again.

Or suppose that you sense a refusal is based on a lack of trust in the church or its leaders, or even a lack of trust in you as the leader or recruiter. You might be tempted to dig for specific reasons and become defensive, even accusatory, in your attempt to "fix" the problem. Don't do this. It will probably close all doors for future relationship and service with this person. A better response might be to say, "You are such a gifted person with so much to offer. If you don't want to volunteer at First Church, I'm sure they would love to have you over at Sunrise Church across town. I'd love to keep you here, but I want you to be where God wants you and will be glad to help and bless you wherever that is." This may give the person an escape route without destroying your relationship. It's also possible this will change their perspective and build some trust. Of course, they may also decide to take you up on your offer and head across town to Sunrise Church. And then they might come back to see you again in six months. Often, those who switch churches wish they hadn't, but a conversation like this, done well, can help both of you avoid burning bridges. Be a bridge-preserver, not a bridge-burner. Even if someone declines a volunteer opportunity, keep the door open.

Volunteers In Waiting

There is a long line of volunteers in waiting—people who are called, gifted, and able to serve. We know this because volunteering is something God designed us to do. It is Christlike and biblical. And it is also popular, something people enjoy doing, regardless of their religious beliefs or faith commitments.

Make yourself aware of the reasons why people volunteer, and the reasons why they don't. You will find many people who are willing to volunteer and are drawn to the opportunities you provide for them, while others are not. Get to know people, take the time to listen to them, and then seek to match their desires, gifts, and schedules to the challenges you are tackling, providing them with work that makes a difference.

2

~~~

Churches Are Volunteer Based

LEITH

"All of your volunteers must be paid," the veteran consultant said. "If you don't pay them, they will quit and do something else."

This sounded like really bad news to me, especially when you understand that our church was short on both money and volunteers.

The consultant went on to explain that *all* workers must be paid if you expect them to do a good job and keep working. But then he clarified a key point. He said that it's wrong to think that volunteers work for free and your staff works for money. No one works for free. The difference between volunteers and staff is in *how* they are paid.

Every good business manager knows that money alone is never enough to retain the best employees. They will consider the benefits, whether their supervisor is competent, how much flexibility and freedom the job provides, and above all, whether they can have a sense of satisfaction in what they do. Several factors contribute to making someone a happy, productive worker. The same is true for volunteers. Volunteers may not receive cash for what they do, but they are still paid—with good relationships, creative training, the resources they need, clear expectations, plentiful praise, and even loving correction. Above all else, though, volunteers should find some sense of satisfaction in the job they do. Though they aren't making money, they still get paid.

The good news is that millions of Americans are willing to volunteer for the paycheck of satisfaction rather than the paycheck of money.

A Nation of Volunteers

America is a nation of volunteers. Global surveys repeatedly list the USA as one of the top volunteering countries on earth. According to the US Bureau of Labor Statistics, 64.5 million Americans volunteer each year for an average of fifty hours spread out over a twelve-month period. That's a whopping 26.5 percent—more than one quarter of all Americans. The bureau defines volunteers as "persons who did unpaid work (except for expenses) through or for an organization."[2] In other words, these stats cover formal volunteer work. They don't count the guy who helps his next-door neighbor take out the garbage every Wednesday. So if you add into all of this the volunteer work that is not done through an organization, the numbers are far, far higher.

The stats we do have tell us that women (29.5 percent) volunteer more than men (23.2 percent). They tell us that adults 35–44 years old are the most likely to volunteer (31.6 percent), and adults 20–24 years old are the least likely to volunteer (18.9 percent). Teens (16–19 years old) have an amazingly high volunteer rate of 27.4 percent, while the rate of volunteering for adults over 45 years old tapers off as age increases. These numbers may contradict some of our stereotypes, namely that people volunteer less when they are busy in middle age and volunteer more when they reach retirement, but the numbers don't lie. Are you married? Do you have children? Married Americans (31.9 percent) are more likely to volunteer than never-married Americans (20.7 percent), and those with children under age 18 (33.5 percent) are more likely to volunteer than those without children (23.8 percent).

Education and employment also make a difference—42.2 percent of college graduates volunteer; 17.3 percent of high-school graduates volunteer; 8.8 percent of those with less than a high-school diploma are volunteers. And those who are employed (29.1 percent) volunteer more than those who are unemployed (23.8 percent). Workers who have part-time jobs (33.4 percent) volunteer more than those with full-time jobs (28.1 percent).[3]

People volunteer for all sorts of different organizations. They volunteer at hospitals, soup kitchens, and animal shelters. They build homes for low-income families, collect toys for children at Christmas, and help supervise after-school programs. They coach soccer teams, lead scouting programs, work with the elderly, and gather signatures for ballot initiatives. Regardless of the work they do and why they do it, one thing is abundantly clear—people are willing to give up their time and energy for the sake of others.

And this is true for the church as well. In fact, it is *especially* true of the church. The US Bureau of Labor Statistics tells us that "the organization for which the volunteer worked the most hours during the year was most frequently religious." Religious organizations lead the list of volunteering opportunities.

Now, if you are a church leader, you might be saying to yourself, "This all sounds great, but why don't we have enough volunteers to keep our ministry going? We continually come up short." You might be tempted to despair or assume that all the good volunteers are going to other churches. If that describes you, I have good news—this book is for you! There are volunteers in your church, but you may not know how to call them out yet. You need to understand *why* people volunteer, *how* to recruit them, and *the way* to keep them. Some churches and nonprofit organizations know how to gather volunteers and retain them over the long haul. Others make mistakes, make decisions that undermine their efforts, and may even chase away their best workers.

The Importance of Asking

So what motivates volunteers? We unpacked this in the last chapter a bit, but let's add to that one last statistic from the US Bureau of Labor research. Volunteers were asked why they became involved with their organization, and the number-one reason they gave (41.3 percent) was because they were *asked* by someone in the organization.[4] Such a simple answer, and yet it is the exact same story you hear from fundraisers when they wonder why people give money. They give simply because someone asked them to contribute. Of course there are good ways and bad ways to ask, but being asked is the primary reason most people volunteer. As James says when he writes about prayer in his New Testament letter to the church (James 4:2), we don't *have* because we don't *ask*.

Volunteering begins by asking people to help, but it also needs to call them to a sense of ownership and responsibility in what they do. Let me give you an example of what I mean.

If you are from an older generation, you might remember a time when the majority of America's major roads were lined with litter. Today, you can still find papers and cups along the shoulders of major highways, but it's nothing like it used to be. In the late 1960s, Lady Bird Johnson, wife of the thirty-sixth US president, made highway beautification her signature issue. Hiring people to pick up the litter was very expensive, so states posted "Do Not Litter" signs that threatened fines of hundreds of dollars for those who broke the law. Sadly, many drivers continued to throw trash out the window right in front of those signs, so lawmakers responded by raising the fines to thousands of dollars. But it didn't help. Litterers are difficult to catch. But there's something else involved. The truth is that there is more to motivation than money.

James Evans from the Texas Department of Transportation addressed the ongoing problem of littering along the highways. Evans recruited volunteers and organizations in East Texas to "adopt" sections of highway and clean up the litter. In 1985, the Tyler Civitan Club was the first organization to sign on, taking responsibility to clean up two miles of US Route 69 between Tyler, Texas, and Interstate 20.[5] And soon the "adoption" program was spreading across the country. Families, churches, businesses, and nonprofit organizations adopted a stretch of the highway and took personal responsibility for keeping that section clean. Today there are tens of thousands of miles of highways adopted by volunteers who periodically pick up the litter. You've probably seen the signs with the names on them. This program has saved millions of dollars. The volunteers have been honored and recognized, and the highways look better. On top of that, far fewer of us litter, because we don't want to dishonor the volunteers who have to pick it up. The Adopt-a-Highway program has spread now to other nations around the globe. It's a simple concept, but it works. And it relies on volunteers.

When we tap into the resources of volunteers, we discover that there are ways to change the world for good *without* spending more money. And what applies to cleaning roads also applies to the ministry of the church. Understand what motivates people. Get creative in your thinking. And then ask.

Churches Are Volunteer Organizations

At their core, churches are volunteer organizations. Even if they can, most churches should not replace their volunteers with hired employees. Sure, there are a few that have tried, but we believe this is the ecclesiastical equivalent of going on hospice—that any church with enough money to pay for all services is a church that is dying. A church without volunteers is an unhealthy church. This is true because the act of volunteering is an expression of worship, it serves people, and it builds relationships. Volunteers are more likely to give generously than those who don't volunteer. So if you want to see your offerings increase, recruit more volunteers. Churches are among the few organizations where the same people are the owners, the funders, the staff, and the customers. And one of the practical reasons that the church of Jesus Christ has continued to exist for two thousand years and has spread almost everywhere on earth is that it is a volunteer organization. Empires, businesses, and armies come and go, but the church remains, led and served through an army of volunteers.

When Jesus first said to his followers, "I will build my church, and the gates of Hades will not overcome it" (Matt. 16:18), he was talking to a group of volunteers, disciples who had left everything to follow him. And when three thousand people were added to the church on the day of Pentecost, they were all volunteers. No one was forcing them to join; they had been touched by the power of God and wanted to belong to God's people.

When Paul embarked on his missionary journeys and started churches across the empire, those churches were composed of volunteers. The New Testament was written to volunteers. The first-century church certainly had some well-to-do Christians in it, folks like Lydia the Merchant, but a majority of the first Christians were poor people or slaves. There wasn't much money to go around, and available offerings were typically used to help the poor, not to hire church staff. In Paul's famous fundraising trip across Greece and Asia, he made it clear that the money raised wasn't for him; it was to benefit the poor Christians in Jerusalem (2 Cor. 8–9). In fact, in 2 Thessalonians 3:7–9 Paul noted that he did not want to be an economic burden on God's people: "For you yourselves know how you ought to follow our example. We were not idle when we were with you, nor did we eat anyone's food without paying for it. On the contrary, we worked night and day, laboring and toiling so that we would not be a burden to any of you. We did this, not because we do not have the right to such help, but in order to offer ourselves a model for you to follow."

The New Testament teachings on spiritual gifts assume that the church is a body composed largely of volunteers. If you define a "spiritual gift" as a "job" or a "responsibility" when you read Ephesians 4, 1 Peter 4, Romans 12, and 1 Corinthians 12, you get a sense of the church and its extensive volunteer system. All Christians have one or more "jobs" or responsibilities that they need to do in order to make the church healthy and effective. God himself decides who does what, and as long as we all volunteer to do the job God has called us to do, the church functions as God intends. Romans 12:4–8 says this well: "Just as each of us has one body with many members, and these members do not all have the same function, so in Christ we who are many form one body, and each member belongs to all the others. We have different gifts, according to the grace given us. If a man's gift is prophesying, let him use it in proportion to his faith. If it is serving, let him serve; if it is teaching, let him teach; if it is encouraging, let him encourage; if it is contributing to the needs of others, let him give generously; if it is leadership, let him govern diligently; if it is showing mercy, let him do it cheerfully."

Protestant churches, in particular, give great emphasis to the New Testament doctrine known as the "priesthood of all believers." The bedrock words of 1 Peter 2:9 are instructive here: "But you are a chosen people, a royal priesthood, a holy nation, a people belonging to God, that you may declare the praises of him who called you out of darkness into his wonderful light." Unfortunately, many Protestants understand this teaching—that all believers are priests with direct access to God—as a doctrine of *privilege*, not a doctrine of *responsibility*. Certainly, it is a privilege to be able to go directly to God without someone else serving as your mediator. But notice that the primary focus of 1 Peter 2:9 is on the responsibility of serving God by declaring his praises. If all Christians are priests, then all Christians have work to do in the church. Every believer is called to serve, voluntarily and joyfully.

Being a Volunteer Means Being Like Jesus

So what does it mean to be a volunteer? Volunteering is not primarily about money. It's not about the budget or the positions that need to be filled. It is primarily about being a follower of Jesus—being *like* Jesus.

Jesus was the ultimate volunteer. As the eternal Son of God, he volunteered to become human and to serve us by dying on the cross and rising from the grave. Jesus declared his purpose in life: "The Son of Man did not come to be served, but to serve, and to give his life as a ransom for many" (Matt. 20:28). As Christians, we seek to become like Jesus, and that means serving others. And serving others most often means volunteering.

This means that churches have a biblical responsibility to help their people serve. When we provide service opportunities, when we recruit, train, and support volunteers, we are actually discipling fellow believers. We are fulfilling our mission as a church by making disciples who make disciples, teaching them to do what Jesus did. We dare not deprive Christians of this, but we also need to help them see that volunteering is a gift from God to help them grow and become like Christ. Even when every volunteer position in a congregation is filled and there is a waiting list, churches should encourage and bless their parishioners by helping them find service opportunities inside and outside of the church. Why? Because volunteering is one of the primary ways that we become Christlike. Serving others in this way is vitally important.

Does this mean that *everyone* in the church should be a volunteer? Should we abolish paid staff and hope that the work will still get done? No, not exactly, although there are churches and denominations that are 100 percent volunteer with no paid clergy or staff. It is possible. But let's take a close look at the Bible. Jesus didn't spend his entire life in volunteer ministry. He spent most of his first thirty years in secular employment, working (we assume) as a carpenter and probably volunteering in his local synagogue. It was for the last three and a half years of his life on earth that he was involved in full-time public ministry and received funds from generous supporters.

And even though the disciples were volunteers, they also received financial support. Peter quit fishing and Matthew quit tax collecting, and along with the other disciples entered full-time ministry. Most certainly Timothy was paid as the pastor of the church in Ephesus. First Timothy 5:17–18 was written by Paul, and while Paul financially supported himself, he also insisted that "the elders who direct the affairs of the church well are worthy of double honor, especially those whose work is preaching and teaching. For the Scripture says, 'Do not muzzle the ox while it is treading out the grain,' and 'The worker deserves his wages.'" In writing this, Paul used the Greek word *timç*, which is translated into English as "honor," but it often refers to money. Paul was making it clear that Timothy and others who worked full-time for the church in Ephesus should be paid a salary.

Today, it is quite common to have a church with at least one or two people on paid staff, usually a pastor and perhaps an administrative assistant. Regardless of how many paid staff positions a church has, the paid positions coexist along with volunteer positions. So how do we reconcile the idea of a volunteer church with the need to compensate some? There is no simple answer here, and it requires a balance that is unique for each local church. The key is in remembering that those who are paid aren't better than the unpaid volunteers, but that the church has decided how to best utilize the resources God has provided.

A simple analogy might help here. Most American fire departments are staffed by volunteers who have other full-time jobs, receive essential training, and are regularly on call for emergencies. But everyone recognizes that the fire department will be more efficient and effective if there is at least one person who is available full time. So the citizens of the community chip in enough money for one of the firefighters to quit his day job and put in more hours at the firehouse. He arranges the schedules, orders supplies, supervises equipment, writes reports, and feeds the dog. The fire department is still based on volunteers, but one of the volunteers is now the captain and is paid. There is a need for a healthy balance—someone who is paid who can serve the volunteers and enable them to volunteer more effectively. If every firefighter in a small town of ten thousand is paid full time, the balance is off. The fire department will soon bankrupt the budget. On the other hand, if there is no one available to put in the extra hours to keep the department running right, the balance is off again. Morale will suffer and mistakes will be made.

In the North American church, as churches have grown larger and more prosperous since 1950, they have added more paid positions. Today, salaried staff do what volunteers did a generation ago. Some of this is the result of increased prosperity. There is also an unhealthy perception, in some churches, that wealthier Christians should pay someone else to do the work, rather than volunteer themselves. In addition, ministry has gotten more specialized, and this has brought remuneration. Churches often hire specialists for required functions, to do everything from playing the organ to servicing the boiler, because no one in the congregation has the needed technical skill. Some larger churches choose to have every department headed by a paid staff person. Others have the musicians in the worship services on salary to increase quality and dependability. In many cases, this works well. In other situations, this mentality deprives volunteers of opportunities to exercise their gifts, fulfill the call of God, build meaningful friendships, and have the satisfaction of serving others.

In recent years, economic downturns have forced many churches to lay off paid staff and increase opportunities for volunteers. Some churches with attendance of less than five hundred are numerically declining and chronologically aging. Economics are changing, and some of the changes are leading to additional openings for volunteers and fewer positions for paid employees. Smaller churches are exploring what it means to call a bivocational pastor, someone who has both secular employment and a part-time church salary.

How should we view these changes? Are they problems or opportunities? We believe that more churches need to embrace these changes and see the opportunities they provide. Paid staff are not always the answer to our need for dependable people with training and skill, though that is often the simplest and easiest solution. But in the long term, the challenges we face won't be solved by money alone. Instead, churches need to develop the discipline to recruit, train, nurture, and retain volunteers, utilizing them as they should and as God intends.

Growing in Wisdom

At a recent church leaders' conference held near St. Louis, the topic under discussion was volunteering. During the question-and-answer session, one of the attendees raised her hand. She said to the leaders gathered there, "All this is well and good, but we try our best and still can never fill all eighty-seven committee positions in our congregation. What, practically, should we do?"

Before answering, the facilitator asked the woman a question. "How many people do you have in your church?" The woman's answer was revealing.

"Fifty-two."

Eighty-seven positions to fill in a fifty-two-member church. Sometimes our problem is not a lack of volunteers; it is effectively training, equipping, and motivating the people God has already provided to do the work God is calling us to do. Sometimes we have the right number of volunteers, but the wrong number of committees. The volunteer church is more than a slogan or a nice book title. It is God's design, and it's the biblical pattern. But knowing that we need volunteers is just the beginning. We also need to exercise good judgment and make wise choices. We need a Spirit-led combination of biblical teaching, leadership support, a volunteer-friendly culture, and courageous common sense.

Are you ready to get started? Turn the page and let's get going.

3

Top Leadership
Must Support

LEITH

Veteran explorer Ernest Shackleton announced his "Imperial Trans-Antarctic Expedition" early in 1914. Antarctica was then and still is an extraordinarily inhospitable and dangerous continent. The recent start of World War I added to the risks of the journey for this British explorer, but the First Lord of the Admiralty, Winston Churchill, gave his consent for the expedition to begin.

One of the most intriguing parts of the amazing Shackleton story is the undocumented account of an advertisement he ran in a London newspaper: "MEN WANTED for hazardous journey, small wages, bitter cold, long months of complete darkness, constant danger, safe return doubtful, honor and recognition in case of success." Even if the ad itself never ran, we know that Shackleton's expedition caught the attention of more than five thousand volunteers, men who were interested in signing up for exactly what the ad promised.

In so many ways, the expedition was a disaster. The ship *Endurance* was frozen into the pack ice until it was crushed and sank. The crew of twenty-eight escaped on three lifeboats and drifted 346 miles to Elephant Island, far from any shipping lanes. In a seemingly desperate last chance for survival, Shackleton took five of his men on a twenty-foot wooden lifeboat and left twenty-two of them behind with the promise that he would come back to rescue them. The lifeboat was pointed toward South Georgia Island, where there was a whaling station with help—a trip of eight hundred nautical miles across freezing, stormy seas. Shackleton and his small crew did eventually reach South Georgia Island—on the wrong side. Shackleton climbed a previously unconquered mountain without climbing gear or mountaineering skills, reached the whaling station, and eventually rescued all of his crew. His journey is one of the most celebrated stories of exploration and leadership from the twentieth century.

There is a seldom-mentioned postscript to the story that is worth mentioning. Shackleton led a follow-up expedition back to Antarctica in 1921. Though many of the rescued crew members from the first journey were never fully paid, and they had almost lost their lives, several of the men volunteered to return with Shackleton and try again. What endeared these men to Shackleton? What led them to *voluntarily* follow him to a place where they risked death and suffering with little chance of reward? Books have been written trying to answer that question. They emphasize Shackleton's calm demeanor in the worst of crises. They mention how he gave his food to another man when they were all near starvation, and that he got frostbite after offering his own gloves to a man with freezing hands. Shackleton was fiercely loyal to his volunteers, and this loyalty created bonds with his men that were worth more than the promise of money and fame.

Several other famous explorers in the early 1900s tried to reach the South Pole. Among them were Robert Falcon Scott, the diligent English scientist who died trying to reach the South Pole; the brilliant Norwegian explorer Roald Amundsen, the first to actually make it to the South Pole; and Edward Adrian Wilson, the physician whose five-man party was second to reach the South Pole just five weeks after Amundsen. Commenting on the different men who attempted this amazing feat, Apsley Cherry-Garrard wrote, "For a joint scientific and geographical piece of organization, give me Scott; for a Winter Journey, Wilson; for a dash to the Pole and nothing else, Amundsen; and if I am in the devil of a hole and want to get out of it, give me Shackleton every time."[6]

Leadership matters. It inspires people to do things—hard things—when they trust their leader. People will follow leaders into the toughest situations and the worst places, and the same principles of leadership that led men to sacrifice everything to follow Shackleton apply to volunteers for church committees, Sunday school classes, and worship teams as well. A volunteer church begins with good leadership.

Volunteering Is Discipleship

A church that values people, that recruits and trains them, that nurtures and rewards them, will end up with more volunteers. But that's not why you do these things. It's not just about getting more people; valuing volunteers is the right thing to do even if you never recruit another volunteer.

Leaders are called to shepherd the people in their churches, to teach them to obey all Jesus has commanded (Matt. 28:20). And as we saw earlier, since Jesus commands his followers to love and serve others, volunteering is an integral aspect of discipleship. It is core to the church's mission. When we teach Christians to volunteer, we teach them to be like Jesus, and that is very good all by itself. It's also why prioritizing volunteers should be woven into the fabric of church leadership and emphasized as a core value, rather than limited to a once-a-year push or a volunteer appreciation Sunday. Some pastors I know can't stop talking about their children, and they seem to work a story about them into every sermon they preach. In a similar fashion, pastors should be constantly talking about their volunteers. Recruiting, multiplying, and training volunteers are central to the discipleship mission of the church.

When God announced the birth of Jesus to Mary, Joseph, and the Bethlehem shepherds, he delegated the job to angels. When Jesus wanted the way prepared for his public ministry, he delegated the assignment to John the Baptist. When Jesus desired for his gospel to be proclaimed in Jerusalem, Judea, Samaria, and all the earth, he delegated evangelism to his disciples. But when Jesus sought twelve men to be his band of apostles, he recruited them himself. Then he spent three and a half years teaching and training them. When he finally ascended to heaven and delegated the advance of his gospel and the building of his church, they were ready to do it.

This is not to suggest that leaders today must do all the recruiting or that there is something wrong with delegating responsibilities to others. To the contrary, most volunteers are best recruited by other volunteers and by those who will serve alongside them. But we do want to emphasize that pastors, elders, and other church leaders must themselves be recruiters and disciplers. This is what we call the Jesus Approach. When leaders value volunteering, it demonstrates to the rest of the church how to relate to volunteers.

Peter, Andrew, James, John, Matthew, and the other followers of Jesus weren't formally trained to be world changers. So how did they do it? Most likely, they taught the way they saw Jesus teach, they prayed the way they heard Jesus pray, and they washed feet the way that Jesus washed their feet. Jesus did not enlist volunteers to do what he didn't want to do himself. When he told his volunteers to take up their crosses and follow him (Luke 9:23), he knew that he would soon be leading the way.

Church leaders who use this approach pray with their volunteers to teach them how to pray, invite them home for dinner so they will know about hospitality, study the Bible with them so they know how to research and understand the Scriptures, and take them along to resolve interpersonal conflicts so they will see how it is done. When a church leader tells a volunteer, "You can call me at home or on my mobile phone any time day or night," that volunteer will probably consider saying the same to those in his or her small group.

Whose Church Is This?

Have you ever heard someone refer to a church as "Pastor Joe's church?" Or describe a famous congregation a thousand miles away as "Hank What's-his-name's church?" I remember a conversation I had in the Minneapolis airport with a fellow traveler who kept talking about his experiences at "Pastor Joe's church." After a few minutes, I asked him, my voice just above a whisper, "Does Jesus know?"

The traveler asked, "Does Jesus know *what*?"

"Jesus thinks it's *his* church."

Okay, the chances of correcting this common theological misspeak are probably slim. But things get a little more serious when Pastor Joe frequently refers to "my church" in the same way he talks about his house or his car. It's downright dangerous when church leaders start thinking that the church is something they own and operate.

A conference was once held in the worship center of one of America's megachurches, and the purpose of the gathering was to honor the thousands of volunteers from that church, along with many others in the same denomination. Shortly after the evening meeting began, the senior minister of the large church arrived and was seated in the front row. The music paused, and he stepped up to greet the people. Though he meant well, his words were not all that wise. To the gathered volunteers, he said, "You are volunteers who make our Sunday school possible, and there's something I want you to always remember when you prepare your lesson, teach your class, and care for your students."

What was this nugget of wisdom, the one thing these volunteers should remember?

"Remember that you are an extension of your pastor. As the pastor of this church, I can't come to every class, so you are my representative." When he finished his speech, the crowd politely clapped, and he left the room.

Is this the message we want our volunteers to hear? That we need them because we can't do all the work ourselves? That they are our representatives, doing the work we have delegated to them? No. This falls short, far short, of what the Bible teaches. Instead, we need them to hear that we are colaborers for Jesus. We serve on his behalf, doing his ministry, for his glory. The truth is that these volunteers *are* the pastors and teachers spoken of in Ephesians 4:11–12, doing the ministry that Jesus did.

I do not say this to disparage pastors who truly love and value their people. But we must never forget that a pastor is a shepherd, and the top shepherd of the church is always Jesus—not the senior pastor. Jesus is the founder, leader, boss, and owner. He is the most important person in the church. It's always "the church of Jesus Christ," never ours to own.

The Seven Suggestions

You've probably heard of the Ten Commandments. Let me add to those ten the "seven suggestions." These are seven ways that church leaders can serve God by creating a church culture where volunteers thrive. These suggestions are for pastors, leaders, elders, deacons, directors, or whatever titles apply—anyone who is responsible for the spiritual and organizational health of the congregation.

1. ASK

While the *tactical* "ask" in order to recruit volunteers usually comes from fellow volunteers, the *strategic* request should come from church leaders. They plant the seeds for volunteering with frequent invitations to serve.

We already know that the primary reason anyone volunteers is because they are asked. So it's safe to say that the primary reason why a person *doesn't* volunteer is because they have not been asked. When you ask, be sure you ask in the best way possible.

Most churches follow a predictable schedule. We all know the stress of a coming event or outreach, or the seasonal need for additional volunteers to run the Sunday school program. Without people to lead the small groups or sing on a musical team, things get stressful. Nine times out of ten, the team leader of the shorthanded ministry will come in desperation to the pastor of the church, days before the deadline. "You have to make an important announcement this Sunday. Tell them we *need* somebody to teach the fifth-grade class, or we're going to have to shut it down this school year—those eleven-year-olds will probably have their spiritual lives wrecked." And so the pastor, with few alternatives, turns up the pressure. He guilts one or two adults to sign up, and the problem is solved for a few months.

There has to be a better way.

When we ask people to volunteer, we should highlight the specific needs of the ministry and how they match with the interests of potential volunteers. The goal is *never* simply to fill a spot with a warm body. When asking, try to get into the head and heart of the volunteer and remember that the Holy Spirit is ultimately responsible for calling that person to teach the class. Explain the opportunity that person has to shape the lives of children. Talk about your own fifth-grade Sunday school teacher and how she impacted your faith. Communicate that you are excited to offer this opportunity to a volunteer.

The leaders in the church need to develop a culture where asking is normal and expected. No more pressured requests, guilt trips, or stress-inducing calls for help. This means working to make the "ask" a normal, comfortable, and healthy part of congregational life. In a healthy marriage, there are constant requests to walk the dog, pick up the kids, or do the laundry. And while some of them can seem fairly routine, they are made in the context of an ongoing relationship. When we ask for volunteers, we want to emphasize the larger relationship, the importance of doing significant work, together, as the body of Christ, each part of the body doing its part.

We also want to emphasize that it is fine to say no or to prefer some opportunities over others. Not all volunteer work is equally enticing to everyone. But that's an important part of understanding and establishing a *culture* of asking. Some family members like dogs more than others, or prefer doing the dishes over doing the laundry. In a healthy culture of frequent asking, opportunities are presented in a way that matches up with the preferences, gifts, and skills of those in the church, family, or business.

You'll be amazed at the power of asking, if you ask in the right way. Compare this to the guy asking his girlfriend to marry him. It's not just the "ask," but the way he does it. Putting the question on the scoreboard at an NFL game may work for some women but alienate others. If he knows her well and loves her much, he'll already have an "asking relationship" and will propose in a way that honors her and persuades her to say yes. The same goes for leaders asking church people to volunteer — know them, love them, and ask in ways that are honoring and persuasive.

You'll be amazed at the power of asking, if you ask in the right way.

2. AFFIRM

We all love affirmation. We like to feel valued, that what we are doing is important. We want to know that our leaders care about us. Leaders in the church can look for a thousand different ways of affirming volunteers. Some are easy and inexpensive; most are completely free.

Start out by always giving the credit to others. Volunteers deserve a lot of credit because they work hard and make churches effective. When pastors and other church leaders hint or imply that success and effectiveness are because of the pastor or the church leadership, this diminishes and demeans the hard work of volunteers. When Paul wrote to the Thessalonian Christians, he began his letter with affirmation: "We always thank God for all of you, mentioning you in our prayers. We continually remember before our God and Father your work produced by faith, your labor prompted by love, and your endurance inspired by hope in our Lord Jesus Christ" (1 Thess. 1:2–3). That's a lot of volunteer affirmation!

Here is a rule of thumb: when leaders affirm volunteers, that affirmation is multiplied by ten in the mind of the volunteer; when leaders criticize volunteers, that criticism is multiplied by twenty in the mind of the volunteer. Volunteers exaggerate the feedback they receive from church leadership, and they doubly exaggerate criticism. A little praise goes a long way, and criticism should come in small doses.

Where to start? (1) Thank volunteers when talking on the phone, passing in the halls, or referencing them in public. Say thank you until it becomes a habit. (2) Set a goal of two handwritten thank-you notes a week. In ten years you will be shocked at how many people will have saved and reread your notes. (3) Think through any necessary criticism of volunteers very carefully and even write out notes before you speak with them. Season your criticism with doses of praise and gratitude, and deliver the criticism in private, not in public. Always give a reasonable and helpful path toward a better way of serving.

3. ADVOCATE

Volunteers want to know that church leadership is on their side and is supportive. While this doesn't mean that leaders always agree or give volunteers everything they want, the volunteers should be confident that their leaders listen to them and stand up for them and their needs.

Let's suppose that two small groups want the same room at the same time for their groups to meet. If a pastor or church board member visits both groups, listens before answering (sometimes leaders are too quick to give a solution without hearing or understanding the problem), and says, "I'm on both your sides and will pray and think and work to find a way to accommodate both groups and leaders," then these volunteers will have hope for a positive outcome. Of course, both leaders also know that two objects cannot occupy the same space at the same time. Even if they don't get exactly what they want, they will know that their concerns are important to their church leaders.

Advocacy means that the top leadership of the church speaks on behalf of volunteers, provides training, pushes for financial support, finds helpers for them, answers questions, and does the little stuff—like unlocking the room that holds the photocopier on Sunday morning.

Advocacy is not slavery, and leaders can't be available to satisfy every whim of every volunteer. The truth is that volunteers don't *want* helicopter leaders who are constantly hovering, watching their every move. But they appreciate real and symbolic actions that assure them that they are being heard. They know the leaders will be there when needed, and that they will have the volunteers' backs.

4. MOTIVATE

Motivated volunteers are amazing to watch in action. They outperform expectations and often do a better job than leaders could have done themselves. But what motivates these volunteers in the first place? Later chapters will provide some practical advice on how to motivate church volunteers. It's a mix of recruitment, training, placement, feedback, gratitude, and support. Once a system of motivation is woven into the culture of a church or volunteer-based organization, it becomes self-perpetuating. Yet there is a simple axiom for church leaders to keep in mind: a satisfied need never motivates anyone. Another way to say it is this: all motivation is based on some level of dissatisfaction.

Let's look at how dissatisfaction works. If you are satisfied to stay in bed on Monday morning, you won't get up and go to work. If you are satisfied with the car you drive, you won't shop for a new ride. If you are satisfied with your marriage, you won't attend a seminar or read a marriage-enrichment book. If you are satisfied with your spiritual life, you won't seek greater discipleship.

Satisfaction can be good, but there is also a healthy need for dissatisfaction in our lives. The good news is that most people have a certain level of frustration and dissatisfaction in their lives! We want our lives to have purpose and meaning. We desire to know God and serve him effectively. We are looking for closer, lasting friendships. We hope to be part of a church that is truly pleasing to God and making a difference in the community.

Good leaders will listen carefully to the discontent of their people and offer opportunities for them to pursue greater fulfillment. To the person looking to lead a life that makes a difference for others, you can say, "You will love the satisfaction of shaping a child's spiritual life through the class you teach." For someone looking for more depth in their relationships: "One of the very best ways to build close friendships is to serve together on a volunteer team for a year." Or for the person who wants to serve others and follow their passions: "When you discover your spiritual gift and exercise that gift, you will have a whole new spiritual experience that will change your life."

Remember that potential volunteers aren't likely to be motivated by the needs of a leader. They won't necessarily be compelled by desperate calls for a volunteer or a warm body to fill a role. They will be motivated

---

Many in our churches run successful businesses, are great teachers or nurses, lead significant civic organizations, or have shown excellence in the arts or on the sports field. Many of them cheerfully stuff envelopes and hand out flyers, but we also should keep in mind broader responsibilities in line with their varied experiences and gifts.

When I recognized that our church was woefully ill-equipped in the area of apologetics, I set out to change that. I could have put together a class or conference and taught all the sessions. But with a host of good thinkers in our congregation, I set out to train experts—six from our congregation. Each would do extensive reading and would prepare a professional presentation related to some of the toughest questions facing Christianity.

Not an easy assignment; these six volunteers read dozens of books and articles over fifteen months. They wrestled with what they read, developed solid outlines, and practiced their presentations. Then they put on the best conference our church has seen in years. Yes, I was there to help them along the way—no good leader drops a task on someone and runs. But mostly I was giving them a vision for what they could do. And they did it. They made themselves into experts the church can turn to for years on answers to tough questions.

—JOHN

---

by their own dissatisfaction and their own needs. A leader matches up the needs of the church with the dissatisfactions, needs, and gifts of the volunteers.

5. ELEVATE

Some churches elevate leaders, and some churches elevate volunteers. The choice leaders make is reflected in who gets the most visibility and recognition. Who do you choose to lift up and elevate?

At Wooddale Church in suburban Minneapolis, there is an analogy we've used for several decades. We compare the organization and the leaders of the church to a human skeleton. Everyone needs a skeleton; we'd all be blobs of formless flesh without one. But when your skeleton shows on the outside, you know you have a serious problem. Most of us never see one of our bones in a lifetime (unless it's in an X-ray).

Think of the board, pastor, leaders, staff, constitution, bylaws, and policies as the skeleton of the church. Absolutely necessary to do the work of the church! But minimize showing them off. Keep them under the skin. What then shows? Volunteers who do the ministry of the church. Think of the volunteers as the skin, eyes, hands, feet, hair, and mouth of the church. Give them visibility. Elevate the volunteers and keep the leadership and organization under wraps.

One volunteer was asked to serve on a church board, and she declined. She explained to us that God had called her to be a personal evangelist, and she didn't want to step down from this satisfying and effective use of her spiritual gift in order to spend time in committee meetings. She'd gotten the right message. Ministry really matters. We need to let those with leadership gifts do what they do so that the much larger cadre of volunteers can get the main ministry of the church accomplished.

6. RESOURCE

If the first responsibility of leaders is to ask, then "resourcing" is a close second. Resourcing means providing what is needed to get the job done. On this list are things like training, books, transportation, meeting rooms, food, computer software, music, guest speakers, and other tools for ministry. And as you might guess, much of this requires money.

The church budget is where leaders make a powerful statement about the importance of volunteers in the church. And church leaders are usually the ones responsible for the church budget. Remember that an army without ammunition isn't going to win the war. A salesperson without a phone or car won't reach the monthly quota. A physician without medicine will see patients begin to die. We all need resources to do the job we've been given.

When money is in short supply, church leaders feel like they are in a crunch. How can the budget for volunteers be *increased* when there is not even enough income to pay salaries and utilities? Sadly, this can become a downward spiral of self-fulfilling prophecies. If budgets are inadequate and volunteers can't do their jobs, new volunteers will not be recruited and ministry will be curtailed. Eventually, the church diminishes and dies.

Sometimes volunteers will pay for their own resources. While this is nice, it can also be counterproductive. The self-funded volunteer tends to feel unsupported by the church, and this can lead to isolation, loneliness, and discouragement. It can also create an unhealthy sense of ownership. Typically, it is better for the volunteer to give her money to the church and for the church budget to resource the volunteer. This way there is a shared sense of responsibility and ownership. We are all in it together!

In addition, understand that budgets are moral documents that are highly symbolic. It's not just about the dollars. If church leaders give a 1 percent increase to help volunteers during an economic downturn, those volunteers know they are important and may actually increase efficiency by enough to offset the increase. On the other hand, to cut a volunteer's budget is to send a negative signal that may nudge the volunteer toward quitting.

When developing the church budget, leaders should ask their volunteers what they need, clearly communicating that the leaders see people and ministry and not just numbers and dollars. Yes, there may be times when budgets have to be reduced, but it should always be in partnership with volunteers who are honored by being included in the decision.

7. PRIORITIZE

In a world with limited time and finances, we can't do everything. Churches always struggle with competing opportunities. Someone must decide what to do and what not to do. That is a primary responsibility of leaders.

It is *always* easier to say yes than it is to say no. It is *always* easier to change by addition than by subtraction.

Leaders who refuse to prioritize will tilt their organizations toward chaos and eventual disaster. Making choices between the good and the necessary is one of the most difficult leadership tasks. It takes a combination of knowledge, wisdom, courage, risk, decisiveness, and prayer.

Whole books have been written on how leaders should lead.[7] But we can cut the complex task of leadership prioritization down to two basic rules:

1. *Fulfill your purpose.* Every church should have a simple, clear purpose statement. I often teach in seminary and church classes, and I tell my students, "When it comes to purpose statements, everyone will start out with an A grade. Every punctuation beyond one period will lower your grade by one letter. Two commas take you down to a C. Two commas plus a semicolon and another period, and you flunk." Keep the purpose statement short — no longer than one well-crafted sentence. Then use this sentence to test every opportunity, budget proposal, and church program with the question, "Does [fill in the blank] fulfill the God-given purpose of this church?"

2. *Go with your strengths.* Every person and every church has strengths and weaknesses. Some will pour resources into what they don't do well and neglect what they are good at. Rarely is that a good idea. If your church is effective in ministry with married couples, but not so good at attracting and ministering to single adults, put your money, prayers, people, and programs into strengthening and growing your ministry to the marrieds. As this grows stronger, you will likely be able to gather resources for a future ministry to single adults. Or maybe the opposite is true for your church. If your church is strong with singles and weak with marrieds, prioritize the singles and deal with married couples later.

Provide Competent Command

Peter Drucker has been called the Father of Modern Management. In an informal gathering of church leaders, Dr. Drucker taught that "there is only one thing that an army always owes its soldiers. It's not comfort, food, or pay. It's not even the promise of survival. The one thing every soldier should always have is competent command."

The lives of those soldiers, as well as the outcome of the war and the future of the nation, all hinge on this one thing: the competence of the army's top officers. This is true for the church as well. God has commissioned pastors, elders, deacons, directors, and other leaders as the "officers" of the church. As those who lead, we need to remember that it's not about us. Our work is about serving Jesus Christ and leading his people. We owe our volunteers competence. And this means that we must pray, study, seek counsel, and humbly make decisions that will serve our volunteers well.

4

Create a Volunteer-Friendly Culture

JILL

"He's so tall. I'm sure he loves to play basketball."

"Her family went to an elite college. She must be so smart."

"He's the senior pastor. He is always talking with people. Of course he's an extrovert!"

We make assumptions about each other all the time. We assume that people should know what we know, do what we do, or think the way we think. But life just doesn't work that way. Sometimes we assume that all those who work in Christian organizations and lead volunteers automatically know *how* to work with volunteers.

Too often this is not the case.

We've met with countless churches and volunteer organizations. And we've worked with volunteers in our own church, and we have seen firsthand that simply working regularly with volunteers does not mean you know what you are doing. Or how to do it well.

A lay leader with the title of Volunteer Coordinator came up to me after a session in one of our seminars. She had seen the word "volunteer" in my job title and thought I might be able to help her. She told me that she was exhausted. She shared that she was the only one finding and

---

Training materials for creating a volunteer-friendly church can be found in the appendixes.

training volunteers for her ministry area. She confessed that she had often thought about quitting and wasn't sure how long she could stay in her current position. Sadly, her story is all too common.

One of the most important investments you can make to insure that your organization is volunteer friendly is to have an experienced, dedicated leader whose primary job is to work with volunteers. This person can even be a volunteer; he or she doesn't have to be paid staff. Either way, it is important that you clearly define this person's responsibilities. In some churches, this individual does much of the volunteer work, or is the primary person responsible for finding more volunteers or for providing training. In reality, however, the primary responsibility of this individual is to help the entire organization — everyone else — better understand how to support and encourage volunteer development.

Creating a healthy volunteer organization requires an all-hands-on-deck attitude. Does your church dream of launching more ministries? You will need more volunteers. Does the pastor dream of having a more effective ministry? You need more volunteers. Does the board dream of growing as an organization? You need more volunteers. Having a staff person or volunteer leader dedicated to the success of other volunteer leaders and staff is one of the best steps you can take toward seeing those dreams become reality.

This won't happen overnight, of course. It will take time, but perseverance and patience will be rewarded when new ministries have been launched, become effective, and are growing.

Assess Your Volunteer Culture

When we launched our volunteer development program at Wooddale Church, our first step was to observe and ask questions. We couldn't execute a plan for the future if we didn't evaluate where we were. Some ministry areas were bursting with volunteers and top-of-the-line training. Some ministry areas would rather hire someone for the job than find a volunteer. We had staff members who saw it as their job to recruit and nurture volunteers, as well as staff members who weren't well-equipped or motivated to recruit and develop volunteers.

Early in the process of establishing our volunteer development program, I met with ministry leaders to talk about utilizing volunteers. I asked them about the volunteers they worked with. I asked them to talk about their favorite volunteer. Who was this person? Why were they your favorite? How did they help you? Several people answered, and then one person sighed. "I don't really enjoy working with volunteers," he said. "I find the whole idea to be a waste of time. I'd rather work alone than have to ask for help, tell them what to do, make sure they do it."

Now, if you love volunteers, this response probably raises some red flags for you. But I saw this honest confession as a revealing opportunity. While it was not the response we had hoped for, it gave us a place to begin a conversation and start a gradual, careful education of our church's leaders. Eventually, they better understood why volunteers are necessary and saw the value in recruiting and training others instead of doing all the work themselves.

Admittedly, this evaluation process can be both tiring and eye opening, even discouraging at times. But it is a vital jumping-off point if you wish to develop a healthy volunteer culture. It may lead to changes in staff job descriptions or a reevaluation of your interview process. The bottom line is this: if you want to create a volunteer-friendly culture, you need to assess your current culture and how volunteers are viewed in the church.

Train and Educate, Again and Again

Volunteers make the impossible possible. They are "the hands and feet of Jesus," and we need to make sure we are doing our best to develop them, training and strengthening those hands and feet so they can be effective in the work of God. We should acknowledge that there is always room for improvement in this. We need new ideas, creative recruiting plans, helpful team-building ideas, and much more.

I remember a meeting I'd had on my calendar that I was looking forward to all week. The lay leaders I had been working with for the past three years were all in the same room. I loved interacting with them. These were some of my most faithful and passionate volunteers.

On this day, we were discussing volunteer development training, and we tossed ideas back and forth. As we began to discuss recruiting, one of the leaders enthusiastically told us how he had managed to get some new volunteers for his area. Another leader turned to him with a surprised look on his face. "You mean *we* can recruit? It's not just the staff that does it?" At that moment, I realized I had failed to communicate something essential to my team. It was a valuable learning experience, and I quickly added that component to our training.

It's because of moments like this that we spend time training. This lay leader had somehow missed the fact that he was free—yes, even encouraged—to recruit help for his ministry area. And how had I missed getting that across? The truth is that it was my job to set him up for success, and that included teaching him about recruiting—that he *could* do it—and then giving him some practical ways to find just the right person.

A week later I received an email from this individual with the subject line "I got a volunteer!" Though our leader training had taken only an hour, that discussion had led to another life changed, another person involved in serving in the body of Christ.

Training is important, but it isn't just a one-time event. Developing a volunteer-friendly culture means thinking about continuous opportunities for training and education. It's easy to put volunteer development on the back burner when your time is filled with prep for the next sermon or planning the next "gut bomb/light strobe/pillow fight" night for middle-schoolers. But if you fail to make training a priority, it will lead you back to the beginning—with an average and less than effective volunteer culture.

This danger was vividly illustrated to me during a visit to my dentist. Near the end of the appointment, I learned that I had contracted a dreaded condition—gingivitis. I had been warned of the danger at my last appointment, as well as the appointment before, and even the one before that. At each appointment, our conversation began with a few questions about my flossing—or lack of it. I tried to avoid giving a direct answer, offering several vague responses. Of course, these answers were typically met with raised eyebrows. After this appointment, however, it finally dawned on me that the dentist could *see* my gums. It didn't matter what excuses I came up with, I wasn't going to be able to hide the evidence. I realized that I had a choice. I could be honest and do something about it, or I could continue to avoid the truth. Even though I knew I had a problem, it still took me four visits before I got serious enough to begin flossing each night.

We all need reminders. Continuing education is essential because we all tend to avoid the truth. Turning your church into a volunteer-friendly culture will take time. And then it will take even more time. The good news is that these training sessions don't have to be complicated or intensive; they just need to happen *regularly*.

Leaders Need Encouragement Too

It's not just your volunteers who need training and encouragement. Leaders need it too, including the leaders of teams.

I recall a certain team of individuals that had worked hard all year. As leaders, we wanted them to know that we had noticed all their time and effort, and we appreciated what they had done. I gathered several of our key leaders and told them to smile and yell when I gave them the signal. We made our best college football tunnel and stood there clutching bags of candy.

When the doors of the room swung open and the team entered, we began yelling, "Great job," "Way to go," "You did it," as each team member was handed an empty cup with the words "Great Job with Volunteers" written on it. The startled and smiling team members walked through our human tunnel as their leaders filled their cups with candy and cheered.

So maybe this sounds silly. It probably was. But it mattered. The team laughed, they smiled, and they stood a little prouder knowing that their work with volunteers had been noticed. It's no small thing to lead a team of volunteers. There are endless emails and questions to answer and schedules to manage. It takes time and effort to recruit leaders, get to know them, learn about their gifts and passions, and work with them until they make a decision. The many things our leaders do are important, and they should be supported and encouraged.

Don't assume that everyone, even a staff member or a pastor, understands how to be a great leader of volunteers. You need to be intentional with your education and training, and you will need to be patient to

Two of us were asked to lead a small group of young adult women. We were roommates then and planned to host this small group in our apartment. We had no idea what to expect. We picked a book that was Bible-based and fumbled our way through, not really sure if we were doing it right or if anyone was getting anything out of the time we spent together.

When December came, we decided to change our structured, small-group meeting time to a Christmas-themed celebration, including games involving candy canes and marshmallows. We ate and laughed and bonded and simply enjoyed one another's company. I always look to that party as a turning point for our group. Something clicked that day and fell into place for the group. Soon we started sharing things about our lives, opening our hearts to even scary, vulnerable places within the safe walls of that apartment. There was usually at least one person a week who needed a tissue box for the hot, cleansing tears that come when you finally let go of something you've held tightly to for fear of rejection or judgment or shame. Instead, we were finding loving acceptance and the words, "You too? I thought I was the only one!"

Over the next year and a half, God brought us through laughter and tears, many trials and triumphs, failures and victories, transforming a group of strangers into sisters. He allowed my friend and me to have front-row seats to the glorious transformations and the realization of Christ's true purpose in the hearts of these women.

—MICHELLE

allow time for each person to grow. Some will catch the vision the first time you lay it out, while others may take longer to catch on. Walk with them and encourage them each step of the way.

Take Time to Celebrate

Volunteers give endless hours to being the hands and feet of the Lord Jesus, and frequently there are reasons to celebrate. One of the most exciting responsibilities you have as a leader of a ministry area that oversees volunteers is rewarding them. You will enjoy saying thank you, and can even have fun exercising creativity as you look for ways to highlight what God has done through their service.

Most people get one birthday party each year. What would it be like to celebrate monthly or even weekly? You'd certainly feel valued and loved. So why not look for ways to hold weekly, monthly, or quarterly events with your volunteers? Look for ways to celebrate them while they are in action. Be on the lookout for ways to celebrate successes. Find out what is going well and acknowledge it. Someone has brought in a new small-group member. "That is amazing!" The little girl who hasn't talked for weeks in Sunday school joined in the interaction today. "That is so good to hear!" "Thank you for what you've painted. It's beautiful, and it's going to add so much to the weekend service!"

Words are powerful. As a leader of a ministry, you have the opportunity to speak truth, give encouragement, and pour love into a volunteer's life. Tim was unsure of himself, only fourteen, and trying to figure out his role in life. But there was something about him. He could talk to people and make them feel loved. His leader saw this and decided the perfect part for him to play would be welcoming new people into the group. The teen was uncertain about this request, but eventually he agreed. Week after week, his leader acknowledged how well Tim was doing. Each week the leader affirmed his ability to welcome new young people and encouraged him, pointing out specifics that confirmed how well he was doing.

After one year of volunteering, Tim was a transformed young man, confident and deeply engaged with his church and those he greeted.

Celebrate right away when you see a volunteer doing well, telling him or her immediately. Watch your volunteer start to love his or her role even more.

Celebrate Strategically

The church is made up of busy people. Don't forget that parents, teachers, nurses, business people, and retirees are all volunteers with their own full schedules. So be strategic in how you celebrate your volunteers so it is more than just a nice idea. Take steps to make it happen. Set a reminder on your calendar if you want to make sure your intentions become reality.

Decide ahead of time when celebrations will happen to ensure they will get done. Put them on your calendar and announce them so volunteers can also get them into their plans. Here are a few practical ideas to consider:

- Write birthday cards with a personal note for your volunteers at the start of each month and make sure they get sent.
- After a retreat or large event, send a thank-you email highlighting all the great things your volunteers accomplished.
- Add "celebration" to the agenda, so each week you and your team can have a conversation about who or what needs to be celebrated.

Being strategic about celebrating ensures it gets done. Mark up the calendar and get into a routine. Your volunteers will love you for it. And they will love their roles.

Being a volunteer in a ministry, whatever the size of the responsibility, can feel like running a marathon. *How much longer? Will this ever end?* At times a volunteer may feel overwhelmed by the regular, relentless commitment in the midst of his or her busy life. This can happen even in the best of circumstances and the most supportive of ministries. This is why a genuine thank-you is necessary when a significant commitment comes to an end, whatever the reason. It is important to celebrate the volunteer's commitment before, during, and after, reminding that person of how much he or she is appreciated.

An ending celebration highlights the efforts of all your volunteers. The words of thanks you give at this time could make the difference to volunteers wanting to stay on and to those who want to return if they must drop out for a while. It's always an encouragement to everyone to hear how an individual's contributions have made a difference.

Planning your celebrations can also make them special by paying attention to details that might otherwise get forgotten. One year, we started our time together in student ministries by sharing our favorite candy and drink. It was a typical icebreaker, soon forgotten. That was back in September. Now our school year was coming to a close, and it was the last night of programming for student ministries. An email had been sent reminding all volunteers to be on time for our last meeting of the season. As hoped, our dedicated volunteers showed up on time. For our final meeting, the room was decorated in true student-ministries fashion — cheap and fabulous!

And we'd added a personal touch to it all. As volunteers walked into the room and each found his or her name, they also found a bowl covering up something. When the time came for the "big reveal," each volunteer lifted up the bowl to find a picture with his or her students — and their favorite candy and drink. Eyes lit up. People smiled, remembering our first meeting together. But things were just getting started. A parent had been invited as a guest speaker, and she shared with the volunteers several prayers she had written about her child in her journal. This mother went on to thank them for all they had done and the impact they had on her daughter's life. She said that they, as volunteers, had been answers to her prayers.

The room was silent when she finished. Many of the student ministries volunteers had tears in their eyes. None of this was costly. These were just simple gestures, but it was the best thank-you a team of volunteers could have asked for. They left that night knowing that they mattered and that all they had done that year had not gone unnoticed.

So say a big thank-you — over and over again, in many different ways, and certainly at the completion of a volunteer's commitment. He or she just may be back next year — if not to your area, to serve in another ministry in the church.

Part 2

RECRUITING VOLUNTEERS

5

Volunteers Recruit Volunteers

JILL

A group of seminary students was firing questions at me. We were talking about working with volunteers and, of course, 90 percent of their queries pertained to the topic of recruiting. How do you find volunteers? Where are they? These are the questions everyone asks. The questions went on and on until eventually they caught on to the answer I was trying to communicate to them: *volunteers recruit volunteers.* Some of them looked puzzled. Some were surprised. Others looked relieved. It made perfect sense, once they understood.

Looking for good volunteers? Start with your current volunteers.

- Five people recruiting is better than one assigned to the task.
- Happy volunteers love their area of ministry and tell others.
- Prospective volunteers seeing your current volunteers in action is the best recruiting tool you have.

Five Recruiters Are Better Than One

Lisa plopped down on a chair in my office and announced she could no longer keep it up. Recruiting every single volunteer for the children's ministry each year was too much, and she was done, ready to quit. She explained that her circle of friends was small, and she couldn't continue asking this same group of people over and over again.

We all have social networks made up of people we know and those we have influence with. These are our friends, family, and coworkers—

the people we do life with. Most of the time, everyone's circle of influence is unique to him or her. When more people are recruiting, more volunteers are found.

So how do you go about getting people you know to help you recruit?

- Send an email to all of your connections with a description of the role you are looking to fill and ask for names of all those who might be interested.
- At your next meeting, give all of your volunteers slips of paper and ask them to write down the names of potential volunteers.
- At meetings, talk with your team about potential volunteers and empower them to go after others.
- Distribute role descriptions to use when talking with prospective volunteers.
- Pray with your current volunteers for new ones to join the team.

Talking about recruiting new volunteers should be a regular part of your conversation with current team members. Help them see them-

When I was asked to be a team leader for a trip to India, I wondered how I was going to prepare the group for an experience I'd never had myself. We would have knowledgeable and trustworthy guides, and all the details for our time in India would be covered. Yet I still felt unsure about getting us ready for a trip that would be full of unknowns.

After much thought, prayer, and counsel, the approach seemed clear. I found time for our group to spend together. I felt the most valuable preparation for an experience undoubtedly stretching us in ways we couldn't imagine was to spend time with one another, to really get to know the people we would be traveling and living with.

In preparation, our team went places together, ate meals together, and prayed together. We heard each other's stories and struggles. We learned how to encourage each other and how to listen. And when we arrived in India, we truly were a team. We didn't just serve those we met in India; we served one another. Investing that time before we left allowed us to genuinely care for one another while we were away.

—MOLLY

selves as part of the process. Let them know they "own" the ministry as much as you do. Let them know it's a team effort, and cheer when new volunteers are brought on board.

Your Best Advertising Is Satisfied, Happy Volunteers

The best advertising any ministry area can have is its own people. They are the most trusted source of accurate information and enthusiasm. It's that way with most things in life. You use the moisturizer your best friend uses because she loves it. You buy the truck your friend drives because he says it can haul the most stuff. You eat at the restaurant your brother likes because you trust his taste buds. When your volunteers love their ministry area, they will tell their friends.

If you sit in a pew at our church on Sunday mornings and watch him, you'll quickly discover that Dan is the most energetic sixty-year-old ever. He loves his volunteer role. He's the first one at church on Sunday morning, and he's the last to leave. He will tell you, if you ask him, how much he enjoys personally welcoming people to the church he believes in and loves. He moves quickly from place to place with a smile on his face, welcoming people, guiding them to where they will be most comfortable. Dan is one of our volunteer ushers.

On one Sunday morning, Dan watched a man take his usual place at church. He'd noticed that this gentleman had been attending for almost a year. Dan would greet him, the man would always sit in the same spot, and soon he had his name memorized. It wasn't long before their conversations lasted longer than a few seconds. Dan would talk about his great love for his work as an usher, smiling as he shared. Eventually he popped the question, "Do you want to be an usher?" The typical, predictable, churchgoing man thought about it for a second, and then he agreed.

Why did he say yes? Probably because he'd been watching Dan, a person who loved his role, and had heard him talk about it regularly. Dan was the best one to represent the job, since he did it each Sunday.

Happy volunteers share stories with others, and they invite them to be a part of what they love. Do your volunteers love their ministry? If so, do you encourage them to share stories about what they do with others?

Give Them a First Look

Those who might be interested in "signing up" to help are often worried about it. They ask themselves questions such as, What if it doesn't work out for me? Do I have the time? Is this a lifelong commitment? What if I hate it? What is the group I will be working with like? What will I actually do? Who is the leader? When does the group meet? How often?

A lot of these questions can be answered by simply inviting the prospective volunteer to see the ministry in operation.

A small warning here: take a moment to assess how your ministry area looks, feels, and sounds before others come to visit. Do you need to clean up? Do things need to be more organized? Take a look around to see whether it's volunteer-inspection ready. If things just don't look that appealing, you have some work to do to get ready for visitors.

We decided to launch a ministry at Wooddale Church called First Look—a sneak peek at what it looks like to volunteer at our church. We believed that it would not only benefit potential volunteers; it would benefit all of our ministries as well. Volunteers could observe the area they were interested in, shadow a current volunteer, read through a role description, and ask any questions they might have. A first look may take a little time, but it's not nearly as much work as training in a volunteer who will end up backing out a couple of weeks later. A sneak peek into the ministry area is a win-win for all involved. It also helps the team stay alert to how things look to visitors and potential recruits.

So what do you need to do, practically, to set up a good first look?

- Have a web address designed so people can sign up for a first look. Provide a space where they can put in their information and check off what areas they might be interested in enough to take a first look. Make it easy so all they have to do is hit *Submit*, and you'll do the rest! If you don't have website capabilities, put together a card with the same information request, and then follow up quickly.
- Talk with a volunteer or staff member and give instructions on how to give the prospective volunteer a tour of the ministry area that's of interest to him or her.

- Print out a copy of the role or job description to give to the volunteer or email it ahead of time.
- Schedule an opportunity for the person to talk with current volunteers and ask questions.
- Send a follow-up email or make a phone call to find out what they thought, answer any further questions, and find out whether they are interested.
- Educate all your volunteers to employ this first-look approach in their recruiting. It's an effective way to invite potential volunteers to find out firsthand whether the ministry is a fit for them.

Encourage your current volunteers to "sell" prospective volunteers on coming on board. The team in place is the most trustworthy advertising you will ever have, and their combined social networks are much wider and more diverse than those of just one individual.

~~~~~~~~~~~~~~~~~~~

Fit the Volunteer, Not Fill the Position

LEITH

I was five years old when I had my first piano lesson with Mr. Willet. My mother and my three older brothers all played the piano, so it was expected that I, the youngest son, would also be a pianist. Though my first few lessons went well, after a month the daily drudgery of practicing became unbearable. My mother tried to enforce it through discipline, but after a year of mutual misery, Mr. Willet gave up and turned this unmusical grade-schooler over to his wife, Mrs. Willet. She tried for a few more years with no further success. Finally, Mrs. Willet sent me home with a note for my parents suggesting that I not come back. I'd been kicked out of piano lessons!

My parents weren't going to give up. Convinced that this was a teacher problem rather than a student problem, they found Mrs. Jones. She was affiliated with an international network of musicians based in England and was renowned as an excellent teacher. She hosted prestigious recitals in her home, and she gave annual exams and awarded certificates.

I was the only one of her students to fail the exams.

After eight years of lessons and three different piano teachers, I still had not completed the second-year piano lesson book. My parents decided that it was time for me to quit piano and move on to tennis.

Why was piano such a struggle for me? What was happening here? I'm convinced that some people just don't have what it takes to be a musician. If a student can't carry a tune, can't clap to the rhythm, won't practice, and plays the piano as if it is a typewriter, it's probably a sign that student should do something else. Always remember that some volunteers will be very good at what they do, and others will not. And just because people are willing does not mean they are capable. Just because the church needs a volunteer treasurer doesn't mean that the potential recruit can actually balance a checkbook. The best place to begin is by surveying the *gifts*, *interests*, and *experience* of the volunteer rather than focusing on the needs of the church. But remember: if you want someone to visit shut-ins and the only person available has claustrophobia ("fear of shut-in places"), this volunteer probably isn't going to last very long.

Marvelous Matches

Good matches are marvelous. In the town of Burnsville, Minnesota, they are matching volunteers to jobs that have usually been done by city employees. The *Star Tribune* reports that "Ron Anderson employs four volunteers in Burnsville's inspections division, residents who have included retired 3M executives, former teachers, retired airline employees, and young adults trying to build their resumes."[8] At least fifty other Minnesota cities are doing the same, saving municipal governments hundreds of thousands of dollars and engaging volunteers with high skill and experience levels. Mary Quirk, executive director of the Minnesota Association for Volunteer Administration, says that "what volunteers are looking for is changing, and right now volunteers really want to have an impact."[9]

Some of these city volunteers conduct follow-up on building inspections, but retiree Nancy Sand gives a half day each week to computer work, scanning and filing documents. Why does she do this instead of driving around to inspect properties? It's the best fit for her experience managing the government relations program for the North Dakota state teachers' association.[10]

Good matches like these mean that volunteers will enjoy what they do and the work will be done well. It's a lesson that churches should take to heart. If you work carefully to match your volunteers to the right ministry, you will get the best results. Mismatched volunteers are unproductive, and they seldom stick around for very long.

The Importance of Spiritual Gifts

The New Testament teaching about spiritual gifts builds a strong case for fitting the volunteer to the position.

Think of a spiritual gift as a job. There are many different jobs to do in a church, and God provides abilities to different Christians to cover them all. The Bible compares the way the church is to work together to the functioning of the various organs and appendages of the human body. Each body part has a distinct purpose and function, but the different parts are not interchangeable. They cannot do each other's jobs (1 Corinthians 12). The job of the heart is to pump blood; it has the ability to expand and contract in order to pump. The job of the eyes is to see; they have the ability to sense light rays and transmit them to the brain. The job of the ears is to hear, so they have the ability to sense sound waves, transform them into electrical impulses, and transmit them to our brains. With each job comes the *ability* to do the job.

Again, these jobs are not interchangeable, yet they are all necessary. Hearts can't hear, and ears can't pump blood. The job assignments and the abilities are perfectly matched. In the church there are some with the job of evangelism, some with the job of teaching, and some with the job of shepherding (Eph. 4:11–12). With each job comes the ability to do the job, and every job is necessary for a healthy, functioning body. Here are several things the Bible teaches us about spiritual gifts:

1. *Spiritual gifts are numerous.* Most of the New Testament teaching about spiritual gifts is found in four places: 1 Corinthians 12–14; Romans 12; Ephesians 4; and 1 Peter 4. Depending on how the gifts are counted, there are at least nineteen gifts:[11]

   - Apostle
   - Prophet
   - Evangelist
   - Shepherding
   - Teaching
   - Exhortation
   - Knowledge
   - Wisdom
   - Helps
   - Hospitality
   - Giving
   - Government
   - Showing Mercy
   - Faith
   - Discernment
   - Miracles
   - Healing
   - Speaking in Tongues
   - Interpretation of Tongues

While there are differing theological understandings about several of these gifts, we should not let those differences hinder us from understanding them.

2. *Every Christians has one.* In addition to understanding what the gifts are, we should recognize that every Christian has at least one spiritual gift, and most have multiple gifts, although none of us has all the gifts (Eph. 4:7; 1 Cor. 12:7, 11). Sometimes gifts do overlap. Just as eyes can "hear" by reading subtitles in a movie, or hands can "talk" with sign language, some gifts can substitute for one another in unusual circumstances. But in most cases each spiritual gift is called to a specific job, just as each human organ serves a specific function.

3. *Gifts are empowered by the Holy Spirit.* Spiritual gifts are *not* the same as talents, although there may be some alignment. Paul explains in 1 Corinthians 12:11 that "all these are the work of one and the same Spirit, and he gives them to each one, just as he determines."

In a healthy human body, every organ does what it is designed to do, and that makes for a wonderful fulfillment of God's design. If one organ malfunctions, the whole body suffers. It's not that we can't live without a hand, eye, ear, or foot, but the ideal is that we have them all and they all do what they are designed to do. Likewise, in a healthy church every Christian has been gifted by the Holy Spirit to do one or more jobs.

Like most, I have a day job doing something that's okay—in reality probably rather impactful. But I feel like a superhero in my volunteer role with an anti-sex-trafficking ministry.

I have served in many different capacities with that effort, and I sit down after work to edit some publications or email a list of people I don't know, hoping to get them involved. It sometimes feels like I have an alter ego, like this is perhaps who I really am. By day I'm working a job, and by night I'm fighting sex trafficking. Even better, I can't stop talking about it. For a time I functioned as a promoter of this organization, and it was incredible to see my friends and family buy into what we were doing because I was so excited. This must be my real calling.

—Andrew

When all are functioning as designed, it is a wonderful fulfillment of God's plan. If an evangelist doesn't evangelize, a teacher doesn't teach, or a helper doesn't help, the church doesn't suddenly die, but it's not as strong and healthy as God designed it to be.

Most of us can tell a story about Christians doing jobs in the church for which they were not gifted or volunteers in positions for which they were mismatched. We understand that there are no perfect Christians, and there are no perfect churches. But what we don't want is a fatalistic acceptance of poor church health. That would be like a patient repeatedly going to the wrong doctor or regularly taking the wrong medicine. We want to get the medicine and ministry right, diagnosing and making changes that lead to health.

Get Your Volunteers Ready and Fit

Physical fitness is rarely about taking one pill, doing one exercise, or eating one food. Usually it is a mix of multiple factors that all contribute to a healthy lifestyle. The church with the best matches of volunteers with ministries will follow an ongoing regimen of healthy fitness practices.

START WITH AN INVENTORY

Some churches have an excess of positions they must constantly fill. They are always looking for new people. Others need new positions added to the list so they can fully release the spiritual gifts God has given to them.

Take an inventory of your church or organization by making a written list. Without naming any individual volunteers, write down every ministry and every position that already exists in the church. Don't add any new slots, but be sure to include positions that are currently filled as well as those that are vacant. Next, categorize them according to your mission statement. You may want to create a spectrum from essential to nonessential. What are the positions that are most needed for the church to exist and fulfill God's mission? What are the positions that could be deleted if absolutely necessary and the church would still continue to exist and fulfill its core purpose? Most churches will probably top their list of essentials with someone who can lead the worship service and/or preach and bottom the list with someone who directs traffic in the parking lot. While both are important, directing traffic is dependent on having traffic, which is usually the result of a well-run worship service. Both roles matter, but one is *essentially* important and the other is not.

Next, list the names of all current volunteers. Include the positions they currently fill, but keep your two lists separate.

These two inventory lists give you a broad overview of the volunteer needs and opportunities in your church. This exercise is relatively easy to do, especially in the 95 percent of churches with 250 or fewer attending the average weekend worship service.

If you are ready to tackle the third phase of the inventory, it would be good to have some help from a handful of wise, knowledgeable church members who are good at keeping information confidential. Without the right group of helpers, this third phase can be more harmful than helpful because you will need to rate current volunteers on a scale from one to five on the basis of how well matched they are to their roles or positions.

I like the idea of starting with volunteers' self-evaluation. Request that volunteers complete a short questionnaire with name, position, responsibilities, amount of time serving as a volunteer, whether they like what they are doing, and rate themselves using the following scale:

1. Perfect match of volunteer to position

2. Good match of volunteer to position

3. Acceptable match of volunteer to position

4. Weak match of volunteer to position

5. Mismatch of volunteer to position

Keep in mind that there may be a disproportionate humility factor in some self-ratings. Especially if volunteers are not receiving frequent feedback and affirmation, they may underrate their value and effectiveness. So be prepared to add some extra credit to their self-scores!

Be careful and prayerful in evaluating volunteers. This is an opportunity to serve them and make them more effective, but do not make this into a time to criticize or condemn. Treat them as you would family members whom you know and love. Give them the benefit of the doubt if there are uncertainties. If a serious question arises (like doctrine, abuse, or incompetence), refer that person and situation to the pastor or top church leadership to handle. This evaluation is to be a simple, kind, and straightforward process of matching volunteers with ministries.

A list of guidelines can be helpful for the small team working on the evaluations. Write your own guidelines, but consider some of these ideas for your list:

- What is the level of excitement about the position? Is the volunteer enjoying it? Is there a sense of serving out of obligation?
- Is the volunteer effective in this role? Are there complaints about the work? Does this person feel inadequate or frequently overwhelmed by the task?
- How long has the volunteer been doing this? If a person is new, you need to take that into account. But if someone has been serving for several years and is not happy or effective, that should play into your rating as well.
- Remember that no one is perfect. And we all go through seasons where we aren't at our best. Are there factors in this person's life right now that could make that person less effective in that position?

The goal in doing this inventory is not to create a class system within your church. It is to serve your volunteers so that you can honestly assess what is best for them and for the body of Christ. That is why you need to do this with wisdom and involve only those who are mature and trustworthy.

TEACH ABOUT SPIRITUAL GIFTS

Ask your pastor to preach a series of sermons about spiritual gifts so the whole church understands the importance of knowing and using gifts in its ministry. The series should be positive and encouraging, assuring listeners that they will experience a positive and enjoyable blessing from God as they serve the church in the ways God designed them to serve.

If your pastor doesn't feel comfortable preaching on spiritual gifts, then propose teaching a six-week class covering the same biblical and practical content. Perhaps the pastor and a gifted lay teacher can team up for the class. In some ways this can be better than a sermon series because of the opportunity for interaction and affirmation rather than just listening to someone on the platform.

Use other channels of teaching to make sure these ideas permeate the entire church family. If your church has email addresses for everyone, send a weekly teaching on spiritual gifts that is short, biblical, and practical. Make some videos interviewing volunteers about their gifts and showing them exercising their gifts. You can even let the videos run on a television monitor outside church services so everyone can watch. Ask all the bloggers, Twitterers, and Facebookers to post about spiritual gifts during a designated month. Have children and adults draw pictures of spiritual gifts, volunteers, and ministries and tape those drawings to the walls in hallways, classrooms, and restrooms. Use multiple methods to get the congregation learning, thinking, and talking about spiritual gifts and about volunteering.

I believe that our emphasis and teaching on spiritual gifts at Wooddale Church was one of our best initiatives ever. Every few years, I preached a series of sermons on spiritual gifts, but when we hosted our Spiritual Gifts Seminar as an invitation-only six-week class, things really began to change. There was plenty of teaching, talking, and practicing in this class, and those who attended were asked to try different gifts and report back. Some were asked to try teaching a Sunday school class one weekend. Others were asked to try evangelizing one person or to try helping one family that week. Others tried giving super-generously from one paycheck. By the final week of the class, there was growing awareness of each individual's gifts, as well as a sense of which were the "not-for-me" gifts. Following the success of this class, we hosted another seminar for a new group and then another and another. I kept leading and teaching these spiritual gifts seminars year after year and watched growing numbers of Christians volunteer with the right fit.

HAVE A LITTLE FAITH

You may get nervous at the idea of telling volunteers that they are in the wrong role. Sometimes the fear is that they will just quit what they are doing altogether, or they will start doing something you don't like and force the church to close the Sunday school and cancel the offerings.

Okay, I admit, maybe that's just a little extreme. But fears can control us, and there is a temptation to think that a little dysfunction is better than no function at all.

This is where we find an opportunity to exercise faith in God's plan. Choose to believe that the church belongs to Jesus, and that he is more committed to the success of the church than is any leader or member. Know that God's plan to match spiritual gifts to volunteer positions is good and right and that it will lead to the best days ahead.

Before you invite volunteers to assignments, ask them to share what their spiritual gifts are and what they would like to do to serve Christ and the church. We've said it before: begin with their gifts and interests rather than with the church's needs.

You may be surprised to find out that many people end up naming a gift and a place to serve that is exactly what the church needs. Over the years, you are likely to find that God brings everything together. We really shouldn't be surprised at this — after all, God knows what he is doing!

For those who don't know their gifts or interests, be ready with a plan to help them. Invite them to attend a spiritual gifts seminar. Or meet with an interested but unsure individual for a fifteen-minute lesson on spiritual gifts, and read through the Scripture lists. Suggest several possibilities for them from what you know of them. Offer to pray for them each day for the next week, and then get back together to talk about what to do next.

REMEMBER TO OFFER OPTIONS

Today, we all expect to have choices. Multiple choices are part of modern living. Fast-food restaurants offer dozens of different beverages. Motels ask whether you want a queen-size bed, a king-size bed, or two double beds. Televisions have so many channels that it takes hours just to punch through the list. We have come to expect choices as a normal part of life.

As a volunteer recruiter, you can say to potential recruits, "You are so gifted. I get truly excited thinking about you as a volunteer. From what I know about you, I've started a list of possibilities. Listen to my ideas, let me know what you think, give them some prayer, and let's reconnect about trying out a few of them." Then you can suggest some options for them to consider. They can join a planning task force, take a short-term missions trip, help in a class for the developmentally delayed, or phone first-time visitors to Sunday services.

Offer them choices, and then offer them a test run. It's like shopping for a car and taking a drive in each of the cars you are thinking about buying. Attend one meeting, go on one trip, attend one class, or make one call. These experiences give volunteers a taste of the work and can help them discover the right match of gift, volunteer, and ministry. Those who would never agree to a one-year commitment may discover a ministry they would not have sought out and turn the page to a great new chapter of volunteering.

HAVE AN EXIT PLAN

Flight attendants on airplanes will tell passengers to look around before takeoff to locate "the emergency exit nearest to you." Teachers tell their students where to find the closest exit in case of fire. High-level executives sign contracts with termination "parachutes" in case things don't work out. It's always a good idea to have an exit plan for the occasional volunteer or position that needs to be terminated.

If the assignment is a one-time deal or a short-term experience, an exit plan may not be needed. There is a natural ending to the volunteer experience, and you can allow that to run its course—unless something goes terribly wrong. But with long-term roles or positions, you may want to have a plan for dealing with a mismatch. If a volunteer is invited to serve a three-year term on the church board and discovers after a month that it is a mismatch, an exit plan is a very good idea.

Good exit plans are prepared in advance. Set up a probationary test period of six weeks or a month and schedule a two-way evaluation discussion. Or you can talk with a volunteer in advance and agree that he or she will switch to another assignment after three months if everyone thinks it would work better. For church boards, a common approach is to set term limits. Time off is required after one, two, or three years.

Exit plans aren't easy to prepare, and they can be even harder to execute. That's probably why so few churches have them. But they can save you lots of headaches and pain in the long run. If there is a practice of providing a path out of a ministry, you will likely find it easier to recruit and easier to fix mismatched volunteers. Most of the time you will never use your exit plan, but when you need one, it is good to have it.

What If My Church Is Missing a Gift?

What should you do if an essential gift is missing in your church? You look around, meet with people, and there appears to be no one in the congregation gifted to do specifically what needs to be done. Or what if there is a church member who is the perfect match for a position but won't or can't volunteer? She is already overloaded. He has a health problem. The church rules have a time limit.

In cases like these, a mismatch may be the only match that works. While it is not ideal, volunteers may be recruited to fill slots for which they are not especially gifted but will still agree to do for the good of the church. Thank God for these generous volunteers! But don't allow these temporary mismatches to become permanent. Set up a plan to pray and continue to search for that perfect match.

Some churches in New Zealand have what American business executives call "outside directors." These are board members who are unrelated to the company who have special skills the company needs. Often they are professors at prestigious business schools, CEOs of other corporations, or retired executives with extensive experience and great wisdom. These outside directors become voting members of the company's board for the benefit of the business. In churches, this is done by borrowing leaders from other congregations, usually in different towns. They probably don't attend the church regularly. They come to all the board meetings, participate in all discussions and decisions, and may even have a vote on the board (depending on church rules). An example might be an outsider with financial expertise or someone who has previously led a church through a major pastoral change; there is no one available in the church with equal skills, so the church borrows these needed gifts.

This approach can apply to other situations as well. Newer, younger churches will sometimes connect with larger, established churches to borrow leaders, teachers, musicians, donors, evangelists, or counselors for six months to a year. These are people who are gifted in specific areas and can make a satisfying investment in a temporary assignment at another church until the congregation grows stronger and has its own members who eventually come forward with the appropriate gifts. These borrowed leaders can help speed a church ahead toward health and maturity when it would have taken five years or longer without them.

But does this actually work? Indeed it does. If you are the borrowing church, the first step is to request a meeting with the pastor and a few leaders of the potential lending church. Talk with them about the potential. Assure them that your goal is not to steal sheep but to reach people for the glory of God. Generally, lending churches are larger and generous, with resources to spare, and led by secure, kingdom-minded leaders.

Should a church expect every volunteer to be a perfect match? Is less than 100 percent okay? Of course. Consider Jesus, the master volunteer recruiter. He brought the wisdom of heaven, the heart of God, and passion to his work. Yet out of his twelve chosen disciples, he ended up with only eleven. Judas was a clear mismatch. And several of the others had serious problems along the way, like Peter's denials and Thomas's doubts. Overall, though, the outcome was eternally spectacular, "that at the name of Jesus every knee should bow, in heaven and on earth and under the earth, and every tongue confess that Jesus Christ is Lord, to the glory of God the Father" (Phil. 2:10–11).

7

Keeping Things Clear, Simple, and Memorable

JILL

For years, Brooke had worked at a camp during her summers. This year, even though the camp didn't begin for a few weeks, she had decided to arrive early and put in some extra time as part of the maintenance crew. She wasn't working for large paychecks, but she knew every penny would help with her college tuition. She also knew she'd have fun connecting with old friends and meeting new staff.

A typical morning started with handing out daily responsibilities. On this particular day Brooke was surprised and intrigued by her assignment. The maintenance director told her she needed to hang bars of soap around the trees to keep the deer away. So she picked up the soap and headed off. As she went from tree to tree, the task of hanging all these bars began to overwhelm her. The trees far outnumbered the bars of soap in her container. Eventually, she began randomly selecting the trees that would smell of Irish Spring during the summer.

After hanging up each and every bar of soap, she reported back to the director, ready for her next assignment. After describing what she had just done, the director's face became rather bewildered. He asked her to show him where she had placed the soap. As she led him around the camp to display her work, the director could no longer keep from laughing. He had intended for her to hang the soap near some newly planted saplings bordering the parking lot, trees that were clearly susceptible to being eaten and destroyed, not mature, established trees. Before long, everyone in the camp had heard the story. It was a great example of the need to be crystal clear in communicating what you want. And, of course, it was a story told and retold all summer long, one she never lived down.

You need to be clear when you communicate your expectations to volunteers. Clear expectations are key to volunteers' success and retention, reducing anxiety and frustration for volunteers and their leaders. And they are best when they are ongoing—reiterated frequently and refined as needed. From the moment a new volunteer is recruited, a leader has the opportunity to set him or her up for success. It can be tempting to immediately hand over all the responsibility and move on. But in truth, when a person is new in a volunteer role, you are just beginning. The volunteers' initial moments with a new role can be the most critical to their success because this is your chance to set clear expectations.

Have Clear Job Descriptions

Don't assume that people will already know what you know. Don't assume they will even know what they are expected to do. Give them a clear job description. These descriptions have a dual purpose. They can be used for recruiting as well as for training. The role descriptions should include the following:

- The title of the volunteer position
- The person to whom he or she reports and the people with whom he or she works
- What spiritual gifts are valuable in this role
- What passions or interests such a person might have
- Time commitment, including ongoing training
- Details about what the role entails, including the overarching goal as well as interim measures of progress toward the goal

This kind of role description immediately creates clear expectations during the recruiting and training process. Volunteers will have many questions and concerns about their new roles, and it's usually because they want to succeed. They wonder if they have what it takes. Simply

Both in my experience as a volunteer and a leader, I've learned that clarity is king. A volunteer who wants to help but doesn't have a picture of what to do or how to do it is left frustrated and discouraged. Clear goals, responsibilities, and expectations from a leader will help any volunteer feel wanted, accomplished, and enthusiastic.

On the other hand, working with volunteers can be highly unpredictable. There's always the risk of a volunteer backing out at the last minute. One year we had nearly a dozen broomball teams led by volunteer captains all geared up for the opening tournament. Ten minutes to game time, and spectators were pouring down onto the ice. And then I'm informed that one of the captains and his team didn't show. Fortunately, one of the other leaders was able to fill in at the last minute, but it was an awkward position to be in and could have dumped ice water (sorry!) on the whole evening.

Had I considered the possibility of a team not showing up, I would have had clarity on how to respond and could have clearly directed my volunteers. Preparation can mean the difference between smoothly adapting to the circumstances or facing a stressful debacle.

—JOHN

talking over a role description with a volunteer can clarify expectations and eliminate much of their initial anxiety.

At one point, I organized a focus group at Wooddale Church to assess how we were doing with our volunteers. We invited several people who had been volunteers for years, some others who were new, and some who had volunteered at one time but no longer did. We heard moving and life-changing stories. We heard stories of community found through volunteering. We also heard a few stories that gave us a pang of regret.

One woman had been enthusiastic about the initial training and felt ready to start. Then, once she actually began the ministry, her feelings changed. She described feeling like she was serving on an island. She had some of the tools that she needed, but she didn't feel truly equipped to do the work each week. She told us that the ultimate reason why she stepped away from her position was that she didn't know where to take her little group for breakout sessions. It was an eye-opener for us to learn that something with a simple solution had been so devastatingly discouraging to her.

As this story illustrates, sometimes it's the small things that make a volunteer decide not to continue. Because of this, you'll want to communicate regularly and invite questions. To make sure information and answers to questions are ongoing:

- Send a weekly email with details for the upcoming week.
- Set up a monthly fifteen-minute meeting with your team members so they can check in, discuss issues or problems, know where to go for information, and share ideas with others on the team.
- Provide a list of instructions to hand out to each volunteer prior to his or her first time.
- Schedule meetings quarterly with key leaders.
- Use a training manual.

Clear expectations and regular communication are foundational to effective and ongoing volunteer efforts. When individuals know what is expected of them, frustrations and anxieties are reduced and great ministry can take place. And don't assume that an issue with a seemingly simple solution is going to be understood by everyone. Make it easy to ask questions and get the required help.

Simplicity Works for Everyone

On a visit to another church, I was struck—and blessed—by the wide diversity among the members. An elderly man with gray hair held the hand of his charming wife as she clutched her cane and walked down the aisle behind a teenager with blue spiked hair. While he found his seat with friends, a mother tried to coax a redheaded toddler out from under a chair. Each person there was so different, but they all attended the same church.

When it comes to the church, diversity is welcome. We encourage it. But how can we engage people of different ages, backgrounds, and walks of life in volunteering? Rather than trying to cater to every personality and age group, keep it simple and straightforward.

- Offer various options for connecting people to volunteering.
- Offer one-on-one time for those who need it.
- Make the next steps in volunteering quick and easy.

A church is full of people of different ages and interests, and many have different communication avenues. Some love social networking, some appreciate handouts, and others check the weekly communication for activities and announcements. Keeping it simple doesn't mean that you adopt a one-size-fits-all approach to communication. Think of the different options that will appeal to these different groups and identify the key connecting points that will get their attention.

1. *Regular weekly means of communication.* Though pastors may cringe to hear this, congregants often read the weekly communication during the weekly sermon. Be glad they are actually reading it! Make sure you've included a quick note about how individuals can engage in volunteering in your weekly communication. Don't assume that people know what to do. Offer an email and phone number, and if your church uses information cards, make sure there is a box to check for further information.

2. *Use video.* Videos will be watched (audiences can't help themselves!), and they are powerful tools for telling stories. Make sure that information on how to get involved with the featured ministry area is clearly visible at the end of the video.

3. *Have handouts available.* When people ask questions about volunteering, they are often uncertain and nervous. Sometimes giving them a handout offers them time alone to think and make the next step without feeling any pressure.

4. *Have an up-to-date website.* We live in a world full of constantly changing technology. Fewer people today read newspapers, and more of us look online when we have a question. Make sure you have at least one area on your website about volunteering at your church. At Wooddale Church we take time every week to go through online requests for information on volunteering. Make sure the people who visit you online know how to find a volunteer role at your church on your site.

5. *A designated kiosk or welcome center.* Have a designated place in your church building where people can go with their questions, including information about volunteering. It doesn't need to be all that

much; just make sure you have a spot for those initial queries and something to hand out.

6. *The importance of social networking.* Online social networking is a good way to get a message out. After all, it's free. You can post videos, links, and pictures of your volunteers in action. At Wooddale Church we are finding that people are starting to visit our church just from seeing what we are doing on various social networking sites. Make sure that you are highlighting volunteer options along with stories of the great things your volunteers do.

When I was the Volunteer Development Pastor at Wooddale Church, I found myself naturally asking those who go through our membership process whether they have questions. I asked whether they recognized their spiritual gifts, whether they had specific interests or passions, whether they had toured the building to view specific volunteer areas, and so forth.

People tell me that they appreciate these questions, and often they lead to more conversations, a tour, and suddenly a new volunteer! We have come to recognize that if we offer something a little more in-depth and a personal connection during these individual membership discussions, we will see an increase of volunteers in the right roles.

We've developed something that makes it simple for those who want or need a little more direction, conversation, or guidance when looking for a volunteer role. We call it the Connection Coach ministry. A Connection Coach is a volunteer who acts as a "concierge" for the church and its members and guests. These individuals are trained to know the various ministries, as well as how to find volunteer opportunities with other Christian ministries in the community and beyond. In addition, they are trained in recognizing and nurturing spiritual gifts. They make great tour guides, and they enjoy seeing people involved in the life of our church. We make it easy for a person to sign up with a coach. Those wanting information can call, email, or sign up online, and we'll work around their schedules to make it simple for them.

Make the Next Step Quick and Easy

Our experience is that people really do want to be involved in a church's outreach—whether raking leaves for an elderly couple or going on a short missions trip to Guatemala—and a whole lot of opportunities in between. They want to make an impact, and they want to find community. They want to be a part of something greater than themselves and related to the kingdom of God at work in the world. As leaders of a ministry, our job is to catch future volunteers quickly when they are excited and ready to be engaged.

Emma was one of those future volunteers. She was bright, capable, and willing. She sat in the pew and heard the enthusiastic announcement about all that was going to be taking place in vacation Bible school. "I can help with that," she thought, and she was ready to jump on board. She grabbed the insert and quickly filled out the information. Days went by, and the days soon became weeks. By the time she received a follow-up email, she had lost interest. Work had become stressful, her calendar for the week of VBS had filled up, and she was now disengaged from the opportunity that had once looked so attractive to her.

Part of making your volunteer process simple is following up quickly so your potential volunteer is not confused, irritated, or unsure of what she or he is signing up for. Quickly get back to any who are the least bit interested while that first impulse is still firing their imagination.

We must also realize that if the process isn't straightforward and simple, we can't expect volunteers to stay engaged very long. A process that is too complex and confusing sends the message that you don't really need me or want me. Think about your experience on a confusing webpage—you're ready to buy something, but a lack of clarity is likely to send you packing.

A few years ago, I was eager to volunteer. I had a skill set developed from my years in student outreach and college ministries. I thought I'd be able to help someplace in a growing Christian organization. So I made a phone call and then sent an email. Weeks went by, and I had heard nothing. When I did hear back, I was sent on to another contact. Another email from me, and again a few more weeks went by. Finally, I heard back, and a meeting was arranged at a coffee shop. I couldn't have been more excited! I explained what I had to offer the ministry. At the end of the friendly conversation, the young man looked at me and said he'd follow up "in a few months." *Months*? I was thinking next week. I never received anything more from him. Instead, someone else was sent to meet with me—yet another hoop to jump through. After several months of attempting to volunteer in a ministry arena where I had experience, I realized that they just couldn't figure out how to use my gifts. I was done.

You need to make the process as easy and simple as possible, or you will lose gifted volunteers.

- Establish clear deadlines for turning in applications.
- Clarify how quickly you will follow up and what the next steps are.
- Have contact information available at any time if questions arise.
- Email or call when you say you will, even if you have to explain a decision delay.

Keeping the process simple encourages more volunteers to get involved, and it communicates a strong message: "We appreciate your interest and want you to be part of the team."

The Power of Stories

You know the type—the people who are always late to movies, interrupting the previews, asking which seats are taken, and spilling popcorn on your lap as they noisily apologize and crawl over you to the middle of the row.

That's my friend.

On this particular day, however, she had a good reason not to be concerned about the time. She was with her husband, and they were going to see the box-office hit *Slumdog Millionaire*. The movie had been showing for months, so even if they were a little late, they figured there would be plenty of good seats left.

Tickets in hand, the couple made their way up the dark ramp, around the corner, and stopped dead in their tracks. Nearly every seat was full. The only places left were right in front. They knew they'd end up straining their necks awkwardly, but it was the only option.

Resigned, the couple sat down. Soon, they forgot about the disappointing seats, getting lost in the movie and the powerful story of love, pain, and triumph. If you haven't seen the film, it's about a boy who was born and raised in a garbage-ridden slum in India. As the final lines of the movie were spoken, my friend cried silently as she gripped her husband's hand. And then they turned to see the entire theater spontaneously standing, cheering, clapping, and wiping their own tears. The audience sat again and silently watched until the last credit rolled.

Moments like this don't happen often, but when they do, they are amazing. And that moment in the theater speaks volumes about the power of a story—filling our imagination, inspiring and challenging us to eagerly watch or listen or turn the pages, wondering what will happen next. Stories run through the lyrics of the music we listen to. They are the reason we make time to sit and share a meal with family and friends.

In telling our stories and listening to others share, we come to know one another. We form and shape our identities, both individually and as a community. So it is no wonder that Jesus' ministry revolved around storytelling. The master communicator knew that a story has the potential to engage people, to call them to action, and to communicate truth in a unique and profound way. Jesus not only taught with stories; he knew how to listen to individuals and help them in shaping their own stories as well.

The power of storytelling is often underrated and frequently overlooked. How can something as simple as a story encourage or motivate a volunteer or align a team? Yet that is exactly what stories can do.

It had been another crazy night in the children's ministry area. After the program's end, kids raced through the hallways and shouted goodbyes to friends as they connected up with their parents. One volunteer in particular loved the energy all around him, and he loved what he was doing. Tonight, though, as he went back into his classroom to clean up, his heart suddenly sank. One of the highlights of the night had been the opportunity to give a Bible to a young boy. Yet there it was, left sitting on the table. Maybe he didn't want it. Or had it simply been forgotten in the bustle of the evening's closing activities? Disappointed, he began putting away the supplies from the night. Suddenly he heard the clatter of small feet, and the boy burst into the room. "I almost forgot my Bible!" he shouted.

Later, this volunteer shared the story with his leader and said, "This is why I am a part of this. This is why I do it." That moment not only was encouraging to the volunteer but also was a great reminder of how God was working in the ministry. It brought great encouragement to the leader as well.

Because our children's ministry leader knows the importance of stories, he often repeats this one. When he sees a weary expression on the faces of volunteers after months of working with that little girl who never stops talking or that boy who can't sit still, he shares a story with them. He wants his volunteers to know that it isn't always easy. Stories have a way of reminding us of the big picture, of lifting our spirits, of renewing our hearts. Stories can help discouraged team members remember why they are a part of this ministry.

Become a Story Collector

When you hear a story and there is a tug at your heart, grab a pen and paper. Don't miss these moments! Even better, have a journal or a file on your computer dedicated to those stories that tug at the heart, and do your best to capture them before you forget. Be a master story collector for your team members so that when they need encouragement, you can quickly find a story to share with them. And be prepared to see God bring stories to you. Pray and then watch with your eyes wide open for these anecdotes; they are being lived out everywhere around you, every day. Retell them to others and spread the encouragement around.

- Send an email with a new story monthly or even weekly.
- Have a time for sharing experiences among the volunteers before a meeting or a training event, highlighting what happened last week.
- Invite volunteers to send in their stories for your emails.

Didn't you love story time when you were in elementary school? And let's be honest, aren't the stories the parts of the message on Sunday that everyone remembers? Stories are the glue that holds us together.

STORIES ALIGN VOLUNTEERS

Stories not only encourage us; they are tools that help individuals and teams align with "the heart of the matter." They can transform a team that is being pulled and pushed in different directions and quickly guide everyone back to focus on their mission. Jesus was the master at reminding those around him of what was most important. In Matthew 18, when the disciples began arguing about who would be the greatest in the kingdom, Jesus quickly captured their attention by pulling a child onto his lap and talking about being humble and having a sincere heart like a child. The disciples, in the midst of that self-centered moment, were quickly led back to the true focus of their ministry—serving others with a humble heart. Whenever people tried to divert his attention with technical questions about the law, or his disciples got caught up in their personal agendas, Jesus used stories to refocus their attention where it needed to be.

STORIES INSPIRE VOLUNTEERS

Narratives related to a particular ministry or outreach shouldn't just remain with that group of volunteers. Some stories need to be shared with the rest of the church. Many volunteers focus their service in a single area. Some love women's ministry, some have given themselves to men's ministry, and others are part of the worship team. But great stories about what God is doing through all the ministries of a congregation are wonderful ways to recruit more volunteers, as well as opportunities to invite prayer for those ministries. Use stories to communicate the successes and the challenges of ministry to the whole church.

- Write up a feature in a weekly communication about a volunteer, highlighting why he or she loves serving in a particular area.
- Do a special feature in the church communication instrument about someone impacted by a volunteer.
- Share a link on social networking sites about the volunteer work your church did at a particular time or place.
- Banner the number of sandwiches made by volunteers for the local shelter on a poster or in a printed piece or on the website.
- Take five minutes out of the worship service once a month to share the stories of lives changed by a volunteer team.

Let stories ricochet throughout your church, encouraging current volunteers and reminding others in your church about the rewards of volunteering, both earthly and heavenly. These accounts also will underscore the fact that the church's ministries impact the lives of those served as well as those doing the serving.

Part 3

VOLUNTEER TRAINING AND CARE

Support, Support, Support

JILL

He's painting the new addition on the church building. She is leading the nursery program. Two more are teaching the new class on being financially responsible. They are all volunteers, and they need to be supported. They should have:

- Tools to get the job done—whether information, materials, or actual tools.
- Someone assigned to check in with each of them periodically.
- A group praying for them regularly to whom they can send prayer needs.

Give Them the Tools They Need

If you've ever (or never!) changed a tire, you know you need the right tools to get the job done. It's the same for a volunteer. For most, this will be their first experience running the café, working in the parking lot, or leading a class, so they will need training. Training will look different based upon the activity or role, but all volunteers deserve some form of preparation.

Initial training for the usher ministry might take only twenty minutes before their first experience, whereas training for volunteers in student ministries may take an hour or more for them to be ready for their first night. When you do the training session, make sure you leave sufficient time for them to ask questions.

Connect newcomers with a volunteer veteran for their first experience. During our focus group time at Wooddale Church, we learned that it wasn't uncommon to find out that a volunteer quit because he or she didn't know where to find something as simple as pencils when teaching a class. While this may not seem like a huge deal, when you are dealing with a room full of individuals who need to fill out a worksheet, a lack of pencils is a crisis moment. Connect them with a current volunteer, or someone who once volunteered, to walk them around, show them the environment and where to find materials they will need, and introduce them to others. Having one person designated to help a new volunteer is one of the greatest ways you can offer support. Down the road and well into the ministry, make sure they know where they can turn for ongoing information and advice.

HAVE A DEDICATED SPACE

Volunteers will need specific things to get their particular jobs done — tape, paper, scissors, glue, markers, keys, computers, copy machines, and so much more. If you want to keep frustration levels low, you'll need to think through the tools and resources that each volunteer needs so your volunteer feels supported. And you'll probably need a volunteer to help make sure all these items are restocked and in good working order.

There was one time during my time of serving when I was struggling with some personal issues, and I felt like I wasn't equipped to lead. Why would God call me? How could I be used? I knew I could never be perfect, but I expected to be pretty close. For months I sat in this delusion.

I went on trying to fight this battle alone and hoping no one would notice. One day I stumbled across 2 Corinthians 12:9: "But he said to me, 'My grace is sufficient for you, for my power is made perfect in weakness.' Therefore I will boast all the more gladly about my weaknesses, so that Christ's power may rest on me." It clicked! I'm not supposed to be perfect. I was trying to lead by myself and forgot about God's grace and power. Although I am weak, he is strong.

"God doesn't call the equipped. He equips the called."

—JOSH

If you have the space and means, you may want to designate an area as Volunteer Central, a place where everyone will find the needed supplies. At Wooddale Church, we redesigned a room on a relatively small budget, asking volunteers to decorate and paint. This little room became our volunteer-friendly operations headquarters. We announced the opening of the new room at a weekend service and invited all volunteers to come and tour this new place. The following Monday morning, one of our faithful volunteers was sitting at the counter at 7:30 a.m. putting together the items needed for her class. She looked up at me and said, "It's so nice to have a place of our own."

Most volunteers don't require their own offices. They just need to know where they can find the resources they need and to have a place where they can turn for support and help. Having access to these tools helps them be effective and successful.

CHECK IN REGULARLY

Have you ever been at a dinner or coffee with someone, and all they did was talk endlessly about themselves? Even if you are a good listener, it's hard not to feel used. On the other hand, there is nothing better than going out to dinner with good friends who ask questions about you and your family, who genuinely want to know how things are going. Questions signal that they care. And volunteers want to know their leader cares. Asking simple questions can be one of the best ways for you to convey genuine support for your volunteers. It doesn't matter whether you ask about the task at hand or their families and day jobs.

Many of our young-adult leaders at Wooddale Church pour their time and vitality into groups of seven to twenty young people each week. These groups have high energy levels, and sometimes there are complex issues they must deal with. Roles like this require support systems, or your volunteers will begin to feel isolated. Some will feel overwhelmed and may drop out. We realized we needed a support system, so we picked two wonderful leaders to be coaches for our small-group ministry for young adults. Their job is to care for the leaders. They meet with each leader, ask questions about their lives and the ministry, and "hear their hearts." The coaches mostly listen, occasionally ask some questions, and then pray with them. Our leaders deeply appreciate this support.

Checking in periodically also allows a ministry leader to be a cheer-leader for his volunteers, offering regular encouragement.

Marian answered each question perfectly during her interview for our student-ministries team. She even had high-school kids. I knew she'd be the perfect addition to our ministry team. As the interview was winding down, I asked if she had any additional questions or thoughts to share. She looked at me and said, "I'm a mom, so I'm fine just doing the 'mom things' and being behind the scenes." Listening to her and picking up on her body language, I realized she was a little nervous about the ministry.

To help her feel more comfortable, I decided I would take it upon myself to introduce her to every student each week so she could learn names. Then I encouraged her to go on a missions trip with some young people because I knew the kids would just love her. Sure enough, she signed up for the trip and did something every great mom would know to do—she packed a carry-on bag filled with snacks and candy. Each night, the students would pile into her room, and by the end of the week, she had a new name: Party Girl. The young ones loved her, and she became one of our best volunteers. Marian continued to work with our youth for many years.

A simple conversation during her interview led me to catch some things I might have missed otherwise. I saw what kind of support she needed—someone to help her adjust to a new, larger role in ministry than what she might have imagined for herself. I knew that I could encourage her, and before I knew it, she was off and running on her own. Remember, this isn't difficult. It just requires commitment and intentionality.

- Be intentional and ask questions, whether in the hallway after class or at a regular sit-down discussion.
- Show up during their time of service to see if they need anything.
- Encourage your volunteers in all aspects of their volunteer roles, both the big and small things.

How Do You Pay Your Volunteers?

My college friends weren't known for being on time, and I was not an exception. But I always made sure I was on time for meetings with my Young Life area leader. I'd sit at the table and wait patiently with my strawberry-banana smoothie while he got his cup of coffee. And as soon as he

> I was a volunteer camp counselor with a cabin of girls who had been work-
> ing there themselves throughout the summer. Now they would enjoy a
> week as campers. We canoed, hung out by the pool, and walked around
> the lake together. But I discovered that what they most needed was one-
> on-one time, when they could share their struggles, fears, uncertainties,
> and prayer requests. Throughout the summer they had spent much time
> listening and counseling their young charges, without much time to share
> their own thoughts and feelings.
>
> It reminds me that our leaders need opportunities to set aside their
> "leader mentality," to honestly share without having everything figured
> out. They need someone to hear what is happening in their lives and pray
> with them.
>
> —BROOKE

took his first sip, the words poured out of my mouth. I'd tell him how this
week Megan let me come over to do her hair before she went to prom. I'd
breathlessly rush on about the new girl who showed up for Bible study,
about the exam I just took that hadn't gone as well as I'd planned, and so on.

Tom would patiently listen to me ramble on for at least an hour. I
was one of his enthusiastic Young Life recruits, and I loved the high-
school students I worked with, even though I missed my family. Looking
back, I am amazed that he took time away from his wife and kids to meet
with each of us, his leaders. At these meetings he'd give us the tools
we needed for further leadership, share feedback on recent reports, and
simply find out how each of us was doing.

And I loved volunteering in the Young Life program under Tom
because he paid me. Of course, I never made a dime. Tom paid me not
with money but with his time and his care.

As we've already stated, all volunteers must be paid in some way. To
reiterate this important concept:

- Listen to them.
- Train them.
- Encourage them.
- Be there for them when they struggle and when they celebrate.
- Pray with them.

Every volunteer must be rewarded and affirmed, and as a leader, you have the opportunity to decide how best to compensate each one.

THE GIFT OF LISTENING

For some, it's listening. For many volunteers, simply having their leader ask them how they feel about their volunteer role means the world. For some, they want to share the exciting news of growth in their small group, and they want to get your high five in response. For others, they need to vent about the parent who never says thank you after picking up his or her child each week from the nursery. Or the kid with the lost look in his eyes who hasn't yet opened up. For some it's talking about what their latest new assignment entails.

Volunteers want to know you are interested in and supportive of their volunteer roles and the jobs they are doing. They need to know you care about what is going on in their lives—in their volunteer roles and at home and at work. They need to know you are present—not simply as an assignment but as a friend, as a brother or sister in the body of Christ—and nothing says it more than genuine listening. They'll know you truly *care* from your expression, posture, eye contact, and responses.

Check in with your volunteers *while they are serving*, making a point to ask them how they are doing with their volunteer roles.

- Find out how work is going and ask about details of their lives outside of volunteering.
- Use email to ask for updates on life in general and on their volunteer roles.
- Texts can let them know you are thinking about them and praying for them, particularly after they have shared something difficult going on in their lives.
- Keep information on pertinent facts about family, work, etc., in mind or in a personal file for each person under your leadership.
- Pray regularly for each of your volunteers.

Bottom line, make sure they all know you are interested in their lives and have been listening. You'll be able to tailor these contacts with them as you get to know each one better and know what best works with individual personalities and characteristics. Genuine care will make it natural and easy to personalize your interactions.

NURTURE VOLUNTEERS WITH ONGOING TRAINING

I can still picture Lillian across the table from me as she shared why she had decided to leave the church's ministry. She had been serving for more than a year, but it was too much now, she said. She felt like she kept making mistakes, and there were constant frustrations. The materials she had set out had been moved, the kids ran around the room, and she had never been informed that she could meet with her group only in certain rooms. She felt like a failure.

One of the most important rewards for volunteers is the satisfaction of a job well done, and that comes when they feel adequately trained and competent to do what they are asked to do. I quickly realized that there was a gap between Lillian's genuine desire to volunteer her time and the lack of success she was feeling.

No one wants their volunteers to fail, whether the failure is real or imagined. So one of the best ways to appreciate and, yes, *pay* your volunteers is to train them. We've covered some of this material earlier, but here are a few reminders:

- After a volunteer has agreed to join a ministry area, set up a time to walk through what the volunteer role entails. Maybe begin with the volunteer sitting in on a session or activity similar to what he or she will be doing. All this prior information and experience builds confidence. It can also aid as an alert to "fit" issues and possibly redirect the volunteer to a different opportunity.
- Those all-important rewards can also come through the training you provide, both at the beginning and ongoing as appropriate.
- A role description can be read and reviewed again as needed. When volunteers understand what is expected, they are much more likely to be successful—the best reward!
- Give a short tour on the volunteer's first day so he or she can find the tools needed and meet the others who have similar responsibilities.

- Tell them who to contact with questions as they arise and what to do in emergencies.
- Pray with the volunteer before that first event begins.

The enjoyment and satisfaction of doing a job well is the fuel that keeps each one on track, serving, and loving it. Good training makes those good feelings more likely to happen.

LOOK FOR WAYS TO ENCOURAGE

Your words have power, they are free, and they matter. Each of us needs encouragement. We need to hear we are doing a job well, and it feels great to have someone notice our hard work and effort. This is especially true for volunteers.

I was asked to address a meeting of our church's Garden Club, a group of men and women who make the grounds beautiful. They care for each plant, tree, and shrub like it's their own. I thought long and hard about what I could give them as a thank-you. I didn't think they'd want another pair of garden gloves, and I couldn't afford a shovel for each of them, so I settled on words of encouragement. As I stood looking out the window into the lovely church courtyard and the plantings this club cares for, I reflected on all the meaningful events and encounters that take place there. I decided I'd ask others in the church how they had used the courtyard and gardens during their time at Wooddale Church. I sent out only one email asking for their experiences, and soon my inbox was flooded.

When I walked into the Garden Club meeting, watching the volunteers smiling and hugging as they greeted each other, I hoped what I was about to say would matter to them. I shared about how the church staff and congregation appreciated them. I explained that I had asked for stories of how the gardens and courtyard had been a part of the church's ministry. I began to read to them from the emails I had received.

- "I led a young girl to the Lord in the courtyard. What a beautiful setting to meet Jesus."
- "I sat in the courtyard and worked with a couple who was about to call it quits on their marriage. It was a peaceful place for them to begin putting the pieces of their marriage back together."

- "I love to have my meetings in the courtyard. It's such a pretty place for my volunteers to gather."

As I read through the long list, I could see tears in their eyes. That day, as the Garden Club finished their meeting, each of them thanked me for what I had told them. They left the room understanding better how God was using them in true kingdom endeavors.

Make a list of each of the volunteers in your care and keep track of times you send a personal note (text, email, Facebook, or even in the mail).

Write thank-you notes highlighting their gifts and abilities and successes.

Share with them how they have grown in their volunteer roles.

Gather your volunteers together regularly and note all the things you see them accomplishing, both as a group and individually.

As you get to know the volunteers for whom you are responsible, you will learn how to tailor the ways you provide encouragement to each.

Give volunteers immediate feedback when you come across something exceptional that has happened in their ministry area. The volunteer will feel great about doing his or her role well, and you'll see a face light up from your encouragement. Words matter.

BE THERE WHEN THEY NEED YOU

Life happens. We all have those days when one is great and the next is a disaster. We need to be there for volunteers in the good times and the bad. We need to celebrate when he announces his son just got engaged, and we need to care for her when she has to put Dad in the nursing home. Being present for them says we care, and we want to know what is going on in their lives. It also shows them ways to reflect the same care and concern for those with whom they are working and ministering.

A phone call from the wife of one of the ushers caught me at my desk. She told me about an emergency medical procedure her husband had just experienced, explained he was doing fine and was now recovering at home. I suggested one of our care pastors could visit him. She said that her husband wanted me to come. I tried to cover the emotion in my voice as I quickly said I would be there soon. As I drove to their house, I kept going over the call in my mind. I couldn't believe a man in his seventies saw a twenty-eight-year-old in a pastoral role, that he wanted me to provide the encouragement he needed right then. But then again, why not? We routinely exchange emails each week, and we talk on the phone regularly, since he runs a large part of the usher ministry. The two of us work together in coordinating and carrying out an important service to the church, so it made sense that I'd be with him in this too.

Yes, church volunteers do need to be paid, and although the type of compensation may come in a different form for each of them, it should not be overlooked. Think of it as an investment with a great return.

9

Trust Your Volunteers

LEITH

There's a difference between teaching something and really believing and accepting it. That's what I discovered when it came to trusting volunteers. You see, I frequently taught the principles of Ephesians 4:11–13: "It was he [Christ] who gave some to be apostles, some to be prophets, some to be evangelists, and some to be pastors and teachers, to prepare God's people for works of service, so that the body of Christ may be built up until we all reach unity in the faith and in the knowledge of the Son of God and become mature, attaining to the whole measure of the fullness of Christ." This passage makes it clear that Jesus gives leadership gifts to some as pastors and teachers, and their responsibility is to prepare the rest of God's people for works of service. If the pastors and teachers do a good job, then the people of the church will volunteer and serve in ways that build up the entire church, resulting in unity, knowledge, maturity, and fullness in Christ. Sounds like a really good deal, doesn't it?

I experienced the truth of this early one evening when I was visiting a sick parishioner in the hospital. After the visit, I decided to check in on another church member who had been admitted to the same hospital, though not with anything life-threatening. When I came into the hospital room, I saw that the patient's bed was surrounded by people from his small group at church. I knew most of the people fairly well and thought of them as good examples of Christian commitment and church involvement.

The group was in the middle of a conversation, but they tucked a "Hi, Pastor" in and kept talking. I squeezed in near the end of the bed and stood with the others. The conversation rolled on without me. In some ways I felt invisible, maybe even a little uncomfortable. Finally I suggested that I should read something from the Bible in my hand. One of the other visitors said, "We already did that."

"Okay," I said. "Why don't we pray together?" That's when another small-group member explained, "We already had a prayer time when we all prayed."

Now, it's not that the group was rude or unwilling to read the Bible and pray. It's just that they had come as a group, as the church, and they had already done these things. They didn't need a "professional" to lead the prayer or read the Scripture. These were mature believers ministering to a friend. And while my contribution was welcome, it wasn't seen as necessary at that point. The group had already done it.

I walked to the parking lot and drove away wondering whether what I had experienced was good or bad. Honestly, I felt unneeded and unimportant. That seemed bad. On the other hand, I knew that these small-group members were providing pastoral ministry to the patient in the bed far better than anything I was likely to do. That seemed really good. I realized that in the mix of emotions I was feeling was a question: *Did I trust them?* Did I really believe that they were equipped and able to care for the person in need? Was I content equipping others to do the ministry of the church and then trusting them to do that work, or did I believe that I was better at ministry and that no one could do it as well as I could?

Who Can Jesus Trust?

If you are a Christian, you've probably been asked lots of times, "Do you trust Jesus?" and the answer to that question *should* be a resounding *yes!* We trust Jesus to be our Savior from sin, our assurance of eternal life, and the Lord of everything in this life and forever. We deeply believe that everything he says is true, that he keeps his word, and that he is 100 percent trustworthy. Of course we trust Jesus.

But *does Jesus trust us?* That's a different question.

When I read my Bible, I see that Jesus trusted John. He trusted his disciple enough to acknowledge him as his best friend. In the fourth gospel (called "The Gospel according to St. John"), the author's name is never mentioned. He is referred to as the disciple whom Jesus loved. Jesus had twelve close disciples, including an inner circle of Peter, James, and John, and one "best friend," whom we know was John. Think about the *risks* of Jesus having a best friend. Yet Jesus had as much right to a special friend as we have. It just had to be someone he could trust with this special relationship.

The first three gospels (Matthew, Mark, and Luke) are called the Synoptic Gospels because they all say pretty much the same things. Years later, Jesus commissioned a fourth gospel to tell the rest of the story. There was a lot of material to work with, and so the author had to be someone Jesus could trust to edit out the nonessential miracles and sayings while including the most important information. There was one writer Jesus knew he could trust, and that was John, who wrote, "Jesus did many other miraculous signs in the presence of his disciples, which are not recorded in this book. But these are written that you may believe that Jesus is the Christ, the Son of God, and that by believing you may have life in his name" (John 20:30–31).

When Jesus was dying on the cross, he knew that he would be unable to fulfill the responsibilities of an eldest Jewish son to care for his widowed mother. He needed someone he knew he could trust with her care, and he chose John. "When Jesus saw his mother there, and the disciple whom he loved standing nearby, he said to his mother, 'Dear woman, here is your son,' and to the disciple, 'Here is your mother.' From that time on, this disciple took her into his home" (John 19:26–27). Some ancient traditions say that all the other disciples fled Jerusalem when a great persecution broke out (Acts 8:1), but that John risked his life to stay behind and care for Mary until the end of her life.

And it wasn't just John whom Jesus trusted. Near the end of his public ministry, Jesus used his authority to commission his followers to evangelize the world: "All authority in heaven and on earth has been given to me. Therefore go and make disciples of all nations, baptizing them in the name of the Father and of the Son and of the Holy Spirit, and teaching them to obey everything I have commanded you. And surely

My junior year in college I was serving as student body president. Thankfully I had a team—mostly volunteers—to fill related offices. As busy as I was, I felt like my schedule was nothing compared with the senior representative, a nursing student who, on top of her rigorous classes, was also preparing for her boards and was a newlywed. To be honest, I was shocked she had even run for student senate. But as the year progressed, I found her volunteering for task upon task. Each time, I wondered how she could possibly manage. But as each deadline arrived, her results spoke volumes. Not only were her assignments always completed on time, but they were executed with excellence.

I began to see that a volunteer's ability to accomplish a goal was more important than how busy she or he might be. This became a crucial lesson in deciding how I would delegate in the future.

—JONATHAN

I am with you always, to the very end of the age" (Matt. 28:18–20). Please don't think that those whom Jesus first trusted with world evangelization were the perfect cream of the crop and several notches above our contemporary church volunteers. The sentence in Matthew 28:17 that immediately precedes the Great Commission says, "When they saw him, they worshiped him; but some doubted." Jesus entrusted the world to a mixed bag of people, a group that likely included some doubters.

If Jesus could trust one of his followers to be his best friend, write part of the Bible, and take care of his mother, then certainly we can and should trust volunteers to fulfill the modern mission of our churches. And if Jesus could trust his followers, even some with doubts, to make disciples of all nations, then we can and should trust our volunteers to do the ministry we are asking them to do.

Trust isn't just a spiritual exercise; it's also pragmatic. The only way the church will ever function, grow, and mature is with some level of trust. No leader is smart enough or capable enough to do everything. Since the local church is essentially, historically, and necessarily a volunteer organization, trust is the fuel that makes the church run. No trust equals no church.

I've heard most of the excuses: "People are untrustworthy." "Put the sheep in charge of the flock, and they'll all go over the cliff." "My church has a shortage of leaders and an abundance of carnal Christians." "You can't and shouldn't trust immature people."

There are some practical, commonsense practices that can turn the trust of volunteers into an opportunity for growth and fruitful ministry in our churches.

Keep the Organization Flat

Some churches are organized like an army, government bureaucracy, or business hierarchy, with layers upon layers of leadership, making the decision-making process cumbersome and time consuming. There are congregational business meetings, church boards, committees, subcommittees, superintendents, directors, and an organizational chart that's ten feet long. Such layered hierarchical structures can sometimes reflect a distrust of the people of the church. There may be an underlying assumption that everyone needs to be supervised and that everything needs to be approved in advance. When volunteers in these vertical hierarchies make their own decisions, they are reprimanded for operating unilaterally. Sometimes they are accused of being lone rangers or not being team players. Volunteers are left with two options: get with the program or quit.

We suggest that the organizational chart of the church be as flat as you can possibly make it. If you belong to a self-governing congregation, this may require a rewriting of the church's constitution and bylaws. In churches that operate under denominational rules of governance, it may not be possible to alter the structure. Still, in all cases, leaders should diligently seek to push authority and decision making onto those who are closest to the actual ministry.

Picture a soccer game. The players and coaches don't get to set the rules. The boundaries and rules of the game were set in 1863 by the Football Association in England, but today's local soccer rules are probably set by your school, community, club, or other association. Within the boundaries and rules, the players and coaches can do whatever they want to win. They don't have to go back to England or to the school board for permission to change players or pass the ball. Think of the flat church organization in a similar way, with the board or committee setting the basic rules for ministry and then giving freedom to the volunteers in that ministry to operate however they think is best.[12]

Let's consider an example. The church leadership may decide to set some of the rules for youth ministry. These can include teaching the Bible, having fun, and staying within the budget. They might also require volunteers to undergo police background checks. Or they might set a policy of having at least two adults in a room or at an activity or require that no car rides are provided for students under eighteen. Within these boundaries and rules, the leaders and students are free to choose many things. They can choose what part of the Bible to study, what social activity to sponsor, and how much money to spend. As long as the volunteers stay within the overall rules, they are free to make decisions without checking with a committee.

This means that churches should draw the boundaries they set thoughtfully and carefully, but also generously. There is a tendency, as with any organization, to add rules as churches and their leaders get older. There's also a tendency to react to a negative situation by writing new rules that will restrict volunteers in the future. But when you react this way, you end up punishing and restricting the next generation for the foolishness of the past generation. If you aren't sure where to draw the lines and how to write the rules, ask a basic organizational question: "Will this set the volunteers free to fulfill their God-given purpose?" The ultimate goal is having good rules that free people to serve others, not restricting them or hampering them from fulfilling their calling.

Start a checklist of characteristics of a healthy volunteer church. List some of the things you've learned that describe how a healthy church relates to healthy volunteers. Here are several to consider.

1. *No surprises.* Surprises are too often used to control and manipulate rather than trust and collaborate.

2. *No secrets.* Secrets frequently poison the well of trust; however, this does not mean that we casually disrespect privacy or break professional confidences.

3. *Keep up regular, open communication.* It's not the other person's responsibility to ask the right questions; it's your responsibility to give the right answers even without being asked.

4. *Provide mutual accountability.* This doesn't mean "lording it over" a volunteer; it means checking up with one another about goals and progress.

5. *Jesus is the leader.* The church is never to become a dictatorship or a fan club centered on a pastor, youth leader, musician, or church board member; healthy churches are all about Jesus and not about human superstars.

6. *Servant leadership permeates the church culture.* Remember that Jesus came to serve and not to be served (Matt. 20:28), and that is the high standard for church volunteers and leaders to follow.

7. *Look for long-term results.* In the parable of the talents, Jesus said, "After a *long time* the master of those servants returned and settled accounts with them" (Matt. 25:19, italics added); churches, leaders, and volunteers are ministering to gain long-term transformation of lives.

Add your own items to this list. Even better, invite your team of volunteers to brainstorm about healthy volunteer relationships and how to maintain them.

How Do You Maintain Control?

Does all this talk of trust and freedom mean that we just set volunteers free to do whatever they please? Won't that result in bad doctrine and bad behavior? Don't we need something to keep things under control?

Let me reassure you. No one wants anarchy or chaos. That's why we have leaders. Leaders are responsible to keep the church together and heading in the right direction so the church can be and do what God wants. Leaders aren't necessarily better or smarter than the volunteers. Leadership is functional, not dictatorial. The function of a leader is to be an agent of the Holy Spirit to equip, enable, and encourage the church to serve the Lord Jesus Christ together as a team.

Yes, it is necessary to have some level of control. And there are two ways to exert that control. There are rules, and there is culture. We need both of these, but culture is the more powerful motivator; it is far-reaching and durable. Rules are the boundaries, and every church needs written rules and guidelines on how to do ministry, clarifying the expectations of volunteers, setting policies for effectiveness, and equipping volunteers to comply with church and civil laws. Rules are important, necessary, and valuable. They should be clearly written and broadly communicated. However, the organizational culture of the church is also important, necessary, and valuable. Culture isn't determined by the rules. The culture of the church is determined largely by a mix of history, personalities, and how people relate to one another. The culture of a church reflects what is valued, what its people enjoy, and what matters as a community of faith. If the culture of your church is caring for children, you will take steps to protect children and other vulnerable persons. Even if there is not a rule requiring it, a volunteer in this culture will instinctively report abuse. The same is true in other areas as well.

As churches grow larger, if they want to stay healthy, they need to have fewer rules and rely more on the culture to communicate what matters. Blessed is the church where biblical values, respect, truth, kindness, and love are woven into the values system until they are the normal way of operating. When a newcomer behaves badly, instead of relying

Vanessa and Josiah recently visited our church. They were greeted warmly at the door and shown the way to coffee and where their children should go. Someone else handed them a newsletter when they entered the auditorium, a volunteer up front welcomed them during worship, and afterward, still another one gave them a thank-you gift for coming. They were impressed by our volunteers, but they had seen it all at the large church they previously attended.

What really made our church seem like a fit were the greetings they received from people with no official role, introducing themselves and getting to know Vanessa and Josiah, and it all felt genuine. It both attracted them and worried them at the same time. They knew that in our smaller congregation, they would never be anonymous. That meant they might be asked to get involved themselves.

Vanessa and Josiah are just like many visitors. They come worried they will be talked into volunteer roles they know nothing about and be asked to do one thing after another until they are overloaded and burned out. It's the story in too many organizations, particularly churches.

Volunteers are looking for some basics: respect, training, connections, and opportunities to make a difference. A little attention and appreciation along the way isn't bad either! Working with volunteers is not mysterious, but it is hard, important work.

—ROB

on a set of rules to respond, the culture of the church will automatically direct and shape the newcomer on the better way. Culture is powerful and usually easy to see — some churches are punctual, and other churches start late; some churches tithe, others are over or under 10 percent; some churches are highly denominational, others seldom mention their denomination; some build up pastors, others beat up on their leaders. Culture is typically self-perpetuating, and old-timers teach the culture to newcomers by what they say and do.

Keep in mind that cultures can change. Changes may come from a major event like a fire that destroys the building or a pastor who dies during ministry. More often, change comes through the long process of teaching, telling stories, modeling behavior, and confronting dysfunction. The best church leaders consciously build a culture of trust in their volunteers. They assume the best of volunteers and regularly remind the congregation to value and honor volunteers and give them the support they need to succeed.

Trust with a Capital *T*

Jesus trusted his disciple Judas with the group's money, but that didn't turn out well. Judas was greedy, and he sold out Jesus for thirty silver coins. We assume that Jesus knew what Judas might do but appointed him as Chief Financial Officer anyway. Trust backfired. If trust failed between Jesus and his treasurer, we shouldn't be surprised when trust fails in our churches. Sadly, it's normal and happens too frequently.

So how should we respond when a volunteer cheats, when a leader is immoral, when a teacher is heretical, or a worker doesn't show up? Follow the example of Jesus. Lovingly confront the person who has been untrustworthy. Remember that Jesus confronted Judas at the Last Supper, but also called him "friend" when he was betrayed in the garden of Gethsemane. Stick with the mission — Jesus didn't allow Judas to stop him from going to the cross and rising from the dead. You can be sad and even angry, but don't let the failure of one person shape your response to others. Keep trusting. Jesus trusted the rest of his disciples and refused to transfer the failures of Judas, Peter, and others to everyone else. After his return to heaven, Jesus entrusted the Holy Spirit to his growing group of followers — young, old, new to the faith, and those who had been with him through his earthly ministry.

I recall one Sunday evening when a renowned teacher of world missions sat in our basement and talked about the explosive growth of the church in distant parts of the world. The number of new churches was in the millions, and the number of new Christians was in the tens of millions.

I asked him if he thought these Christians and churches were all doctrinally orthodox—"Do they believe the right things in the right way?" To my disappointment, he answered no, adding that many, if not most of them, had problems with heresy.

Then I asked him what he thought would happen in the future. He told me that it took the early church about four hundred years to confront heresies, establish the doctrines of the Trinity and the atonement, and to narrow the canon down to the sixty-six books of the Bible. Next, he asked if I was willing to give these new churches and Christians fifty years to get it right. He said that as long as they had the Bible and the Holy Spirit, they would eventually become orthodox in their beliefs and practices.

What impressed me most was that this theologian and historian had such great trust in God and the Bible.

You and I are called upon to trust God and the Bible. Together, let us believe that Jesus Christ is the Lord of the church and that the Holy Spirit is at work in the lives of volunteers. Will there be challenges, agonies, and ecstasies along the way as we lead congregations of fellow sinners who have become Christians and volunteers? Of course! But let us have a deep confidence in the great good that God is doing through the church of Jesus Christ and the volunteers with whom he is blessing our congregations.

10

Teams Are Tops

LEITH

The Lone Ranger is often seen as the classic example of the solitary hero. This iconic American character is fictitious, of course—based on the story of a Texas Ranger and told on radio shows, television series, comic strips, and Hollywood movies. But not even the Lone Ranger is alone. He always has his Native American friend by his side. Tonto and the Lone Ranger are a *team*.

Most people, when asked to volunteer, will gravitate toward opportunities to serve as part of a team versus serving alone. And the younger we are, the more likely we will prefer teams. Sociological studies show that while older American generations tend to place a strong emphasis on individualism and finding fulfillment on their own, today's youth prefer team-based opportunities. Many have been on teams since preschool—T-ball, soccer, music camp, class assignments, and church projects. They celebrate team victories with team trophies. In college, they study for exams with fellow students and make reports with classmates and receive a group grade. The whole idea of playing, working, thinking, or ministering alone is uncomfortably strange for them.

In the past, many churches focused on recruiting individuals, often for solo ministries. But that is changing. Churches today are changing their approach to recruitment by recruiting teams of people. They recruit people into team-teaching, worship teams, short-term missions teams, and church leadership teams. Some are even changing the traditional names for these ministries to emphasize the team dynamic, no longer calling it the elder board or deacon board but the leadership team.

Are Teams Biblical?

The word "team" shows up only once in our English Bibles, so a search for the word isn't very helpful. In the one place it does show up, it is used to describe a team of horses, but the concept of teams made up of people is woven into the Scriptures from Genesis to Revelation.

A practical rationale for teams is found in Ecclesiastes 4:9–12:

> Two are better than one,
>   because they have a good return for their work:
> If one falls down,
>   his friend can help him up.
> But pity the man who falls
>   and has no one to help him up!
> Also, if two lie down together, they will keep warm.
>   But how can one keep warm alone?
> Though one may be overpowered,
>   two can defend themselves.
> A cord of three strands is not quickly broken.

As the writer of Ecclesiastes points out, teams make better sense. Two are better than one for many reasons, and three are even better. But even beyond the practical reasons why teams make sense, there is a strong theological rationale for serving as a team. This is clear when we read 1 Corinthians 12:14–26:

> Now the body is not made up of one part but of many. If the foot should say, "Because I am not a hand, I do not belong to the body," it would not for that reason cease to be part of the body. And if the ear should say, "Because I am not an eye, I do not belong to the body," it would not for that reason cease to be part of the body. If the whole body were an eye, where would the sense of hearing be? If the whole body were an ear, where would the sense of smell be? But in fact God has arranged the parts in the body, every one of them, just as he wanted them to be. If they were all one part, where would the body be? As it is, there are many parts, but one body.
>
> The eye cannot say to the hand, "I don't need you!" And the head cannot say to the feet, "I don't need you!" On the contrary, those parts of the body that seem to be weaker are indispensable,

and the parts that we think are less honorable we treat with special honor. And the parts that are unpresentable are treated with special modesty, while our presentable parts need no special treatment. But God has combined the members of the body and has given greater honor to the parts that lacked it, so that there should be no division in the body, but that its parts should have equal concern for each other. If one part suffers, every part suffers with it; if one part is honored, every part rejoices with it.

In this passage, Paul teaches the Corinthian church several important principles of interdependence and responsibility. He refers to the church as a body—the body of Christ. And using the metaphor of a human body, he explains how each part of the body has a specific function and role, and that the different parts all need one another to function the way God intends the body to function. They are dependent upon one another, but they are also responsible for one another. If one part is suffering, the whole body shares in that. If one part is honored, the whole body shares in that. There are no Lone Rangers in the church, either. Just one big team.

We find examples of teams throughout the Bible. Moses was part of a ministry team that included his colleagues Joshua, Aaron, and Miriam. Jesus recruited a core team of twelve disciples with a broader team of 120. The Jerusalem church organized a financial management team of Stephen, Philip, Procorus, Nicanor, Timon, Parmenas, and Nicolas. Paul's missionary team changed over the years but included Luke, Timothy, Silas, John Mark, and others. While essentially unlike anything we can humanly imagine, God is also a team of Father, Son, and Holy Spirit. And though many of the Bible's books are named after individuals, there are plenty of team titles as well, including Judges, Corinthians, Galatians, Ephesians, and Thessalonians.

Let there be no doubt that the Bible is a team-filled book. So what does this emphasis on teams mean for our volunteers?

Three Advantages of Volunteer Teams

Many of the advantages of volunteer teams are self-evident. You might think that these are no-brainers, but it is worth remembering them. All too often, these evident advantages are forgotten or ignored.

1. TEAMS TEND TO BE SELF-RECRUITING

Imagine a team of adults working with a group of thirty-five middle-schoolers. The usual recruits for middle-school ministry are either single adults or the parents of twelve- to fifteen-year-olds. These people all have circles of friends with similar interests—singles know other singles; parents know other parents.

When the number of middle-schoolers in the ministry grows to fifty, there is suddenly an opportunity to recruit more adult leaders. Your team of sponsors gets together and decides to recruit four more adults. So who are your best recruiters? Obviously, those already on the team. They know the responsibilities, and they have relationships with others who are likely to say yes and do a good job. There is no need for another church committee to go looking, and you don't need to make an announcement in the church services or publications. The pastor should not need to worry about finding these volunteers.

The same process works when adult sponsors quit. Mom or Dad accepted a new job out-of-state and needs to be replaced in the middle school ministry. They are sad to go because they have strong friendships and have enjoyed a satisfying ministry. But they can't just leave; they want to be sure they are replaced by others who will do a good job. It's more than a sense of obligation; it is loyalty to the team. So they are the primary recruiters of their replacements. An old-fashioned and far less effective approach would be to make a list of all individual ministry roles supervised by a committee not already involved with these middle-schoolers. This list of roles is individualized and presented as a list of jobs rather than an invitation to join a team. The volunteers may have a sense of loyalty and accountability, but it will be to their personal role and position in the organization, not to the others on their team. When more volunteers are needed to fill another role, they will not see it as their responsibility. They will expect the supervising committee, staff person, or pastor to fill it. Self-recruiting teams are the far better approach.

2. TEAMS HAVE GREATER RETENTION

Frequent turnover is seldom good in any church ministry. Relationships are built over time, and ministry effectiveness increases with experience.

When tenure is short and turnover is frequent, recruiting becomes more difficult. Potential volunteers are reluctant to accept an assignment where the last few volunteers quit after a few weeks or months, meaning that the current volunteers are all new.

Most of us will stick with our team if we feel we belong to the group, even in the midst of challenging circumstances. We've all heard stories of soldiers in war zones who describe their intense connections and deep commitment to members of their own unit. Some go so far as to say they didn't agree with the war being fought or respect the commanding officers, but they were willing to risk their lives to support a fellow member of their squadron. It's the same with church volunteers. We want volunteers to love the church and respect the pastor, but their greatest love is often for those on their ministry team.

Volunteers are happiest and most productive when they are challenged, but not overwhelmed. If there is no challenge in the work they do, a volunteer may quit from boredom or from feeling useless. On the other hand, if the job is overwhelming, the volunteer may quit from fright, inadequacy, and exhaustion. Teams bring balance—challenging one another to do better and sharing the load so no one is overwhelmed. This balance keeps volunteers coming back, and coming back means retention and continuity.

3. TEAMS SOLVE PROBLEMS

Even with the best of leaders, problems are usually better solved by a group than by an individual. Teams share ownership of the current challenge; no one has to handle something alone. They test solutions in advance, and this advance analysis reduces mistakes. They provide a sounding board for leaders; even when there is a supersmart leader with really good ideas, the leader better hones those ideas when explaining them to team members and hearing their questions and responses. Teams help manage mistakes. Whether it is a novice or a veteran who trips up, the team is there to give support and correction.

Teams or Committees?

Ministry teams have become the norm in newer, younger, and nondenominational churches. Established churches, older churches, and churches governed by denominational requirements tend to have a supervisory committee structure.

Supervisory committees are designed to give guidance, support, and accountability to volunteers in the church. Committee members are usually elected by the congregation or appointed by the church governing board. Most have a term limit of three years, and then the committee member must take one year off before returning for another term. Committees have chairpersons who report to the church board or may be members of the church board. In larger churches there often are staff members assigned to each committee. Most committees meet on a monthly schedule for one or two hours.

There are several advantages to traditional committees. They have recognized power and authority to advocate for the ministries they supervise. If a Sunday school teacher is frustrated by a broken radiator in her classroom, she can contact the Christian Education Committee and get the backing of those who can get the radiator fixed and paid for. Committees are interconnected with the broader ministry of the congregation, which reduces "silo-ing," when each ministry of the church is independent from other church ministries like a farmer's silos. This is often evidenced in separate fundraising and budgets, separate branding and publications, and activity calendars that are disconnected from the other programs of the congregation.

Despite these advantages, there are also disadvantages to the way supervisory committees work in some churches. Committee members may agree to serve out of duty, or they are seeking power. They may not have any particular interest in or commitment to the ministry that is being supervised. One church had a building committee chairman who loved the power of his position, yet he declined to contribute any money to the construction of the church building he helped to design. Too many church committees have members who are not personally involved in their area of supervision or have been out of that ministry for more than a year. And committees can easily become advocates for yesterday's traditions and opponents of tomorrow's innovations.

Ministry teams are similar to supervisory committees in some ways. They are composed of church members who have responsibility for oversight of a ministry area, guidance of volunteers, management of finances, advocacy for their ministry, and accountability to the rest of the church. The difference is that they are the people doing the ministry—the teachers, sponsors, musicians, builders, fundraisers, small group leaders, greeters, hosts, parking lot attendants, auditors, prayer warriors, counselors, and other volunteers. They supervise themselves, not as individuals but as a team.

While both approaches can work well when done wisely, we believe that ministry teams are clearly the best fit for volunteers. If your church opts for a traditional committee structure, try filling the committee with volunteers who are currently working in the ministry that the committee supervises. You can even make it a requirement of committee membership. Anyone who drops out of volunteering in a ministry should be expected to resign from the committee. This will enable you to retain the advantages of having a committee while tilting the committee in favor of the volunteers.

If your church opts to use ministry teams for its structure, you will still need to have organizational rules. Each team should have a one-page charter specifying the mission, goals, and responsibilities of the team. The ministry team should regularly report to the church board and/or the congregation or pastoral staff. Annual reviews of team effectiveness are always a good idea, and you should have very clear rules about how money is received, budgeted, accounted for, and spent. This should be written in advance and understood by the team.

Equally clear rules should be established about the recruitment and behavior of volunteers. For example, the church may require that all adults volunteering for youth ministry be Christians, church members, and have a criminal background check before starting. Rules may include a requirement that no volunteer may travel alone in a car or share a lodging (hotel room on a field trip, tent on a camping trip, room in a house during an all-night party) alone with anyone under the age of twenty-one.

Who should write these rules? The place to start is with the volunteers in the ministry because they know best how everything works and may be clearer and more demanding. However, other volunteers and staff in the church should be consulted to cover special topics like financial accounting or state laws about working with minors. The goal in doing all of this is not to create a burdensome list of dos and don'ts; the goal is to lay a foundation for safe, godly, wise, and workable ministry. For those who are just getting started, go ahead and get started, then make revisions every three months for a year until the guidelines are good, workable, and clear for everyone. Annual revisions are also helpful. Keep the list to a few pages. This increases the likelihood that the rules will actually be read and implemented instead of getting filed away somewhere. The longer the list, the greater the likelihood that it will not be used.

The Problems with Teams

A church leader once said to me, "My wife should work for NASA because she can think of everything that could possibly go wrong." Yes, things go wrong, even with teams. Sometimes things go wrong with committees too. And your volunteers will make mistakes. If your goal is to avoid every possible problem, you will never do anything. There is always some risk in anything you do. But some risks are worse than others. Take ten minutes to talk about some of the potential risks in your ministry. It may help you avoid potential problems down the line.

One of the difficulties of working with teams is that they can perpetuate dysfunction. On the positive side, teams are good at recruiting and training volunteers, and they tend to be self-perpetuating social organizations. But if a volunteer team is engaging in sinful or otherwise dysfunctional behavior, there is a strong likelihood that it will propagate that sinful dysfunction. Don't let this scare you away from teaming up volunteers. It's part of the nature of being in community with others. The church itself has this same risk. It's easier to avoid the spread of dysfunction if you address it at the beginning rather than trying to cure it once it is established. Work hard to carefully choose and fully train your teams. If health is established at the outset, health will likely be perpetuated.

Some teams grow corrupt. If corruption sets in, it acts like mold, spreading everywhere and ruining everything. It is very difficult to remove corruption from a ministry team because people are connected to one another. There are often long-term friendships. Addressing this takes strong, courageous leaders willing to purge this corruption. Sometimes leaders attempt this and are forced out for trying. There are many resources available for dealing with pervasive heresy, abuse, embezzlement, and other sinful issues, but the short and simple prescription is to have organizational transparency throughout all volunteer ministries and your entire church organization. Open meetings, open books, open conversations, and open accountability brings light and life. Bright sunlight and open windows are the best ways to prevent and eliminate the mold of corruption.

Teams can become exclusive. It's another function of self-perpetuation. If the team is composed of rich people, it will probably recruit more rich people. If the team has a lot of fifty-year-olds, it will probably recruit more volunteers in their fifties. If the team has mostly newcomers to the church, that's what the team will tend to look like going forward.

Sometimes this type of self-perpetuation is very good. A team of hardworking, highly effective, godly women and men who attract more of the same is wonderful. What we want to avoid is an exclusivity that keeps good people out. Teach the volunteer teams that their ministry is not just to fulfill their program but also to recruit, teach, and develop new disciples for Jesus Christ. They should be looking for recruits who are not exactly the same as themselves. Diversity in the mix of men and women, extroverts and introverts, new Christians and mature Christians, rich and poor, young and old, more educated and less educated, plus diversity of race and Christian experience can strengthen everybody and make the church and the team ministry better.

Team Talk: Four Suggestions for Leading Happy Teams

Here is a short list of leadership suggestions that will make volunteer teams healthy, happy, and attractive to new volunteers.

1. *Set clear expectations.* Uncertainty and ambiguity are the enemies of all volunteers, recruiters, and teams. Be clear about what is expected and how everyone will know if there is success.

2. *Connect teams with other teams.* Meeting and interacting with multiple volunteer church teams can spread health and effectiveness. Let teams visit and observe each other's ministries. Seeing how others

volunteer can be even more helpful than reading books or attending conferences.

3. *Communicate*. Regular communication is essential to keep and develop volunteer teams. Keep it short, frequent, varied, and personal — emails, texts, phone calls, social media, a quick coffee. Welcome questions and comments, and always reply quickly. Volunteers who think you are tracking with them (even when they know you can't be physically present) will listen, love, respect, and keep on volunteering.

4. *Celebrate*. Just about everyone likes a party, and everyone loves recognition. Rather than isolating individuals for praise and gratitude, try to give recognition to the whole team with special focus on individual team members for anniversaries or excellent service. Give the team time to honor members, and give individual members time to honor the team.

The team approach has revolutionized church planting in America and missions initiatives overseas. In past generations, a lone church planter was sent into a community to start a new church, going door-to-door looking for recruits; solo missionaries or couples were sent to a foreign country to find a home, learn a language, and build relationships in isolation. The results were high failure rates in ministries and emotional casualties among ministers.

Modern church planters are assigned to teams with veteran coaches and friends who move into the new town along with the church-planting pastor. Missions agencies now send three families to establish a new outreach in pioneer territory. Stories of success have skyrocketed, with more lasting churches and lots of new Christians. We all do better on teams. Even Adam didn't do well running the garden of Eden as a solo entrepreneur; God said, "It is not good for the man to be alone" (Gen. 2:18). Adam and Eve became God's team.

We could paraphrase what God said and apply the words to our churches: "It is not good for volunteers to be alone." Go teams!

11

Attention to Detail

LEITH

DuPont chemical engineer Sebastian J. Barbarito once famously said, "The difference between mediocrity and excellence is attention to detail." Getting the details right is especially important when you are engineering new chemicals. Sodium (Na) has atomic number 11 on the Periodic Table of the Elements. Magnesium (Mg) has atomic number 12. You might not think there is much of a difference between 11 and 12. It's just a minor detail, right? But if you ignore these "minor" differences you'll find your chemistry lab in flames.

Details matter.

Attention to detail is not chemically explosive when you are working with church volunteers, but it will make a difference. Let's consider something simple, like remembering names. My name, Leith, is an uncommon first name, which means it is easy to get it wrong. If I receive fundraising mail that starts out with "Dear Keith," it usually gets thrown away. Even worse, I once received a letter addressed to "Sister Leith Anderson." When you're a guy, you don't want to be called sister. That letter went in the trash, unopened.

In many Asian languages there is no *l* sound and there is no *th* sound. When you have a name like mine, that means there isn't much left to say. And I've also encountered some who just change Leith to what they know. I've been called Leif and have seen countless misspellings of my name that switch the *i* and *e* around (Lieth). None of these details are huge, unless your name is Leith, and then these details are really important.

I say this to remind you that volunteers are people, not just numbers on your spreadsheet or recruitment list. They have names, lives, jobs, families, birthdays, and all of these details are really important.

Church leaders should be aware of a common mistake when dealing with people: don't confuse what is important to you as a leader with what is important to the people in your church and community. A pastor or staff leader at a church may count church attendance as a very significant detail; the truth is that most others probably don't care all that much. The youth-group sponsor may prioritize stopping for pizza on the way home from church camp; the parents probably prefer that he skip the pizza and get back on time. Good leaders not only pay attention to details; they give attention to the details that are important to others.

The Grand Vision or the Small Details?

Suppose you're a church leader. What matters more to you, the grand vision for the ministry or the details? Which do you say is most important? Don't answer! As you likely guessed, this is a trick question. Both of them are important. Let me give you an example of what I mean.

Eastern Airlines Flight 401 had a very clear vision: to fly 163 passengers and seventeen crew from New York to Miami on December 29, 1972. The airplane was a four-month-old state-of-the-art wide-body Lockheed L-1011 TriStar with a highly experienced cockpit crew. In many ways it was the best of the best—a sunny destination aboard a premium aircraft under the control of a top-notch crew. Then a problem arose. A bulb burned out on the landing-gear indicator light, and the pilot, copilot, engineer, and technical officer all started working on fixing the light, yet no one paid any attention to the autopilot setting. At 11:42 that evening, the aircraft crashed into the Florida Everglades at 227 miles per hour. There were ninety-nine fatalities and seventy-seven survivors. The final report from the National Transportation Safety Board listed the cause of the crash as "the failure of the flight crew to monitor the flight instruments during the final four minutes of flight, and to detect an unexpected descent soon enough to prevent impact with the ground." In addition, they noted that "preoccupation with a malfunction of the nose-landing-gear-position indicating system distracted the crew's attention from the instruments and allowed the descent to go unnoticed."[13] Sadly, while the crew was paying attention to one detail, they were neglecting another. Details matter. But some matter more than others.

Churches flourish when they have a clear vision of what God is calling them to be and to do. The vision of the church is to fulfill Jesus' Great Commission to make disciples. But that's a big vision, and without careful thinking about the details of how to make that work, it's little more than hopeful imagination. Details are important, but they need to be tied to the vision. When there is no vision, the details are little more than busywork. Both are required.

With regard to your volunteers, your vision is clear: honoring Jesus Christ through the ministry of people who serve others as volunteers. To make sure this happens, there are many details. Let's start the list by talking about relationships.

Nurture and Reinforce Relationships

You want Jesus to be honored through the ministry of your volunteers as they serve others. Volunteering is about relationships, about people serving people. Church volunteers are motivated by their relationships with God, the church, other volunteers, and those they serve. There is a key to all of these relationships: how the volunteer perceives she or he is treated by those in church leadership, particularly the volunteer team leaders.

It's important to regularly reinforce volunteer relationships. This reinforcement can be either formal or informal. Formal reinforcement comes through group meetings, celebration events, publishing names of volunteers online or in church publications, and other periodic actions for all volunteers in the church. Informal reinforcement comes through hallway conversations, calling volunteers by name, asking how their ministry is going, offering to help, remembering the topics of previous conversations, and becoming friends. Both formal and informal reinforcement can strengthen all of the relationships on the motivator list. Here are a few ideas to get you started:

1. Have a pastor's sermon that teaches that the church runs on volunteers, then have the team leader remind his volunteers that "the pastor was talking about you!"

2. Pass out stickers that ask, "Have you hugged a volunteer today?" along with hints in advance for volunteers to give each other hugs and thanks.

3. When the Sunday school teacher is on vacation, ask the substitute teacher to have everyone in the class sign a thank-you note to their regular teacher and scan a copy to send to that teacher's smart phone.

4. Send a text saying, "Great to volunteer together with you, but we're really volunteering for God."

The list could go on and on. The point is that relationships grow strong through a thousand little interactions, words, and experiences. Strong relationships grow strong volunteers. One of the best compliments any volunteer can give is to say, "I'm not always sure they care much about me at work or in the neighborhood, but they know and love me at church. Volunteering at church is my favorite part of the week!"

Have a Philosophy of Ministry

Healthy churches have carefully prepared and communicated philosophies of ministry. They have prayerfully and thoughtfully decided who they want to reach and how to reach them. Decisions are made on the basis of the philosophy of ministry rather than random responses to every opportunity or problem.

To give an example, let's consider something basic like the use of church facilities. Believe it or not, this is a philosophy of ministry issue. Some churches have a philosophy that the building, parking lot, church van, and other church property are for the people of the church and not for outsiders. Other churches have a philosophy that God has called them to serve the outside community and make facilities available to the community and even to other churches in the community. These different philosophies will determine whether the church will provide space for community elections, welcome funerals or weddings for outsiders, or host the annual high-school awards dinner. Different philosophies of ministry may determine the design of the sign out front, the way ushers dress at services, and how much the pastor uses "insider talk" that outsiders don't understand or care about.

Volunteers need to know and agree with the church's philosophy of ministry and understand how to apply the philosophy to their assignments. Are Sunday school teachers educating primarily the children of church members, or are they supposed to recruit children into their classes from unchurched families? When volunteers rake the leaves or paint the siding for elderly residents in the neighborhood, are they expected to invite the senior citizens to the church, or should they assume they will stick with their home church? Are neighborhood Bible study groups restricted by the sponsoring church's doctrines, or are they open to the beliefs of other traditions?

There are no clear right and wrong answers to these questions because the answers depend on the context and calling of the church and the way volunteers think about their ministry.

Being consistent is a positive value at home and in the workplace, and it is also necessary at church. Volunteers want to know the philosophy of ministry of the church and may need some help learning how to apply that philosophy in their area of ministry. As a leader, you need to help them avoid becoming legalistic, turning the ministry philosophy into a burden. A good ministry philosophy should empower people and coordinate the diverse ministries of the church toward a common mission.

Keep It Legal

Volunteers often don't know much about the legal matters related to volunteering. It isn't that they don't care about the details of the law; they just don't know. If your church wants to do everything right and avoid breaking the law and inviting lawsuits, you will want to cover some basic legal details.

If your church belongs to a denomination, you likely can ask officials at your regional or district offices or the national headquarters. They may have trained advisors who can explain some of the details of keeping your volunteer ministry within legal guidelines. Churches with or without a denominational affiliation should consider talking with their insurance agent or an insurance company representative for advice.

I mention insurance because it is a good place to begin thinking about legal issues. Start with some basic questions. Does the church have adequate coverage for accidents? Is there malpractice insurance for staff? Are volunteers covered for health care if they travel overseas on a short-term missions trip? (Does their health insurance cover them outside the USA? What about Medicare?) Does the church policy have directors and officers liability coverage for volunteers on the church board?

Another key issue that you will need to address relates to children. Every church has a responsibility to train volunteers to be aware of the signs of abuse and to know what to do when a child or another individual speaks to them about an abusive relationship or incident. Mandated reporter laws vary by state and country, but they are on the books across America, Canada, Europe, Australia, and other countries. The church has a responsibility to inform volunteers about the mandated reporting in their state or other jurisdiction. These laws may also require abuse to be reported to the police (or other government agency) by anyone who has regular contact with vulnerable persons, such as the disabled, senior adults, and children. The abuse may be sexual, physical, financial, or simply neglect and endangerment.

Another legal issue you may need to address is related to copyright laws. These are laws that regulate photocopying of music, projection of films to church audiences, and quotations from authors in sermons or teaching materials. If you have volunteers serving on a worship team, involved in evangelism, or teaching ministries where they utilize video, or teachers who copy handouts or use curriculum, you will need to speak to these issues. Churches should be examples to other organizations by honoring the ownership rights of others and paying fees that are required. But the reality is that most volunteers are not very aware of copyright issues. They may never think twice about running fifty photocopies of sheet music for a church singing group and probably would be surprised if you told them they are stealing.

Permission forms are another area that you should address. These are typically forms that volunteers will gather from parents for church events. Often these require some initial work but can be rather routine once the form is created. Still, it is important that your volunteers understand why some information is important, what the forms are for, and what permission they give to a volunteer leader. If church volunteers are taking a youth group on a camping trip, tubing down a river across town or in the next state, or working on a construction project, they need to know when and why they should get permission from parents in advance of the trip.

Make Sure You Follow Up!

Anyone who has ever volunteered knows the importance of timely follow-up. When questions are quickly answered and their requests receive a rapid response, a volunteer feels valued and respected. At the other extreme, unreturned phone calls, forgotten requests, unanswered emails, and ignored questions will quickly infect volunteers with discouragement, disillusionment, frustration, and even anger. Leaders who fail to follow up with volunteers are a primary reason why volunteers drop out.

If church leaders consistently say they are too busy to respond to emails, this may be a warning signal that they need help. If they are too busy to respond to emails, they probably shouldn't be supervising volunteers. Remember, overseeing volunteers takes time and commitment, and poor leadership with a lack of follow-up will quickly destroy an effective ministry. While everyone goes through seasons of busyness, consistent patterns of neglect need to be addressed. Quick counsel for a troubled leader is needed before volunteers begin to feel disrespected and alienated.

There are different ways you can engage in follow-up, depending on which question or request is being handled. When a question more broadly applies to multiple volunteers, it can be addressed through a weekly email to several volunteers. There may even be specific mention of the name of the volunteer who asked the question or raised the issue. (Be cautious about broadcasting anyone's name; it's usually best to ask permission first.) This honors the inquirer and also shows other volunteers the right approach to raising concerns. When the question or request is more individual and routine, answering once or twice a week usually works (especially when the answers come on Monday night to follow up on weekend questions). If the issue raised by the volunteer is

We were excited about our new volunteer opportunity—tutoring children after school. Our family arrived and was checked in at a desk, and then we waited. Eventually a woman came and greeted us, then told us what we'd be doing. She said we could read with the kids, help them with homework, or play computer games with them. The information didn't seem all that clear, but she walked back upstairs, and I saw her only once or twice in the three months we were there.

We walked into a room of students with nothing but a folder that had reading-grade sheets in it and a pen. We stood there looking around awkwardly until I decided to sit down with a young girl and listen to her read. I would help her with the difficult words, but other than that I simply listened. This is what most of my volunteer hours looked like. While I loved the kids and enjoyed spending time with them, I was disappointed by the lack of structure. I didn't really know what my role was, didn't go through training, and felt useless most of the time. Even when I asked questions about what I should be doing, I never received a clear answer.

I believe this organization could have more volunteers stay longer if they added some structure and training to their volunteer program.

—CARLEIGH

complicated, confrontational, critical, or urgent, a face-to-face meeting should be scheduled as soon as possible.

The most important follow-up with volunteers might not be simply responding to what they ask. Think of it first as feedback on how they are doing. Volunteers shouldn't need to ask how they are doing. Recruiters, supervisors, leaders, team members, and those being served by the volunteers are all positioned to provide thanks, evaluations, and suggestions. None of us wants to be left alone without knowing whether we are on target. All of us want to hear others say, "Thank you!" Most of us would rather not ask and are doubly grateful when the feedback is unsolicited. When the feedback is regular, thoughtful, constructive, and relevant, it makes for a better volunteer and better outcomes.

Doctrine: Know What You Believe

Doctrine is the teaching and beliefs of the church. It's an important detail! Without doctrine, the church isn't a church.

Unfortunately, the word is sometimes misused or misunderstood. Well-meaning church people have said, "Doctrine is divisive, so let's not talk about it," or, "Our church doesn't get into doctrine; we just love God, love people, and teach the Bible." It's true that doctrine divides people and groups, because doctrine includes belief in God, and some people believe in God, while others do not; it's true that doctrine divides, because some believe and teach the Bible, and others do not. For people to say that their church doesn't get into doctrine because they simply love God, love people, and teach the Bible isn't really a solution, because all of those are doctrines.

Doctrine is what we teach. Doctrine is what we believe. To be a church presupposes having beliefs and teaching those beliefs. Let's hope that those who contend that doctrines are divisive really mean that their church believes the Bible but allows for Christian freedom on teachings that are uncertain and open to legitimate differences among serious Bible students.

Some beliefs are widely accepted by all believers, while others are more specific to particular denominations and traditions. Statements like the Apostles' Creed are broadly held by Christians and are recited in unison as part of many church services. Virtually all denominations and the vast majority of local churches have their own creeds or doctrinal statements. Most denominations and churches that include membership require formal agreement with certain creeds or doctrinal statements. Some of these are short, a page or less; some are covered in entire books. Some break down their beliefs into essential doctrines that Christians must hold and optional doctrines or areas of potential disagreement. For example, the doctrine of the Trinity or the doctrine of salvation through Christ are essential beliefs of all Christians, yet various churches may differ on the practice of tithing or frequency of church attendance.

Volunteers who hold positions of teaching or communicating the church doctrines should be informed of the details and committed to holding to the standards the church has adopted. Obviously, this includes preachers, pastors, and board members, but it also should be required of Sunday school teachers, pastoral counselors, and writers of curriculum and other church documents.

That said, some churches will have room for openness and flexibility for volunteers in positions that do not directly teach or supervise doctrine. They may welcome unbelievers as volunteers in certain roles as part of the outreach and evangelism vision for the church. For example, a church may run ministries where volunteers tutor students in English as a second language, offer legal and tax advice for those who are poor, sing in a Christmas choir, serve food at a church supper, stuff envelopes for a mailing, join relief efforts following a natural disaster, or provide a pontoon boat for a summer outing. While an unbeliever could serve in one of these roles, the church should avoid placing in teaching roles unbelievers or those who do not agree with church doctrine. When in doubt, use common sense.

Provide Good Working Conditions

Working conditions can make or break volunteers. Classrooms with comfortable chairs, solid tables, good lighting, attractive walls, and clean floors make for happy volunteers. Lack of technology, cold quarters in the winter, hot spaces in the summer, and a shortage of snacks can make your volunteers want to quit.

Obviously, this raises questions about money. Should volunteers provide their own supplies with their own money? In some cases that can be good to do, as long as there is an understanding about who pays for what. And it is usually better for this to be something that is communicated to the entire team, rather than to individual volunteers. Still, we recommend having volunteers give their contributions to the church and then having the church adequately budget for classrooms, supplies, food, transportation, technology, and other resources.

What if the working conditions are inadequate and there is no way for the church or the volunteer to fund improvements? The worst approach is to keep quiet and let the volunteer suffer. It is far better to acknowledge the problems, talk about changes that can be made without cost, and dream together about long-range changes. This interaction can strengthen the church-volunteer relationship and provide solidarity moving forward. But it shouldn't be a one-time conversation. When working conditions are less than best and advances few and slow, let there be frequent dialogue so that the volunteer doesn't feel alone and abandoned. It is amazing how much we can endure if we sense group concern and support.

Most churches can provide good working conditions. The place to start is with a ministry team of volunteers who meet, pray, think, plan, and work together to determine what is needed to fulfill their mission. Visiting a few other churches that are doing well is a powerful tool in dreaming and planning. Then, write out a few pages of specific plans and a financial proposal to turn your plans into fulfillment.

Church budgets are powerful statements of church priorities. Adding $100 or $1,000 or even $1,000,000 to a church budget to help volunteers do their jobs communicates something about the importance of the work they do. Setting the budget and communicating the dream is an effective way to increase offerings to meet the budget. If you find that the budget is consistently falling short and an appropriate increase can't be adopted, try some other creative approaches. What can be deleted from the budget so volunteer support can be added? Should money be borrowed for the needed building now, rather than waiting until enough money is saved? What about a separate financial fundraiser outside of the budget?

Pay Attention to the Calendar and the Clock

Volunteers are usually busy people. Most of them have full-time jobs, families, and lives outside of their involvement in the ministry of the church.

Serve your volunteers by providing them with advance calendars, limiting the number of meetings you have, and starting and ending your meetings and ministry times on schedule. These simple details are gifts that keep on giving. It can take some discipline to do this, but it helps your volunteers plan ahead and actually increases their faithfulness, expanding their effectiveness. Today, with internet-accessible computerized calendars, it is easier than ever to schedule a year or more in advance. Just take an annual calendar and plug in all your volunteer dates, training sessions, and social gatherings, including the planned starting and ending times. When the first draft is finished, send it to your current volunteers for review and adjustments. Schedules for summer, Christmas, and school breaks may need modifications. When the calendar is updated, send it to current volunteers with a note that says there will probably be adjustments along the way but this is good for beginning. This also helps as you are recruiting new volunteers who frequently want to know when things are happening. With the year's plan in place, your new volunteers know what they are getting into.

Sensitive church leaders are always asking volunteers how the clock and calendar are working for them. Pay attention to the length of church services and whether they start and finish on time. If a volunteer is caring for children in the nursery or teaching teenagers in the park, a simultaneous church service that is longer or shorter than predicted or is frequently unpredictable from week to week creates a problem. It also signals to the volunteer that the church service is what matters, not their volunteer work. Never forget, the clock communicates something to your volunteers, and it can have multiple meanings.

Be a Student of the Local Culture

Culture is the way people relate to one another. And every culture is different.

The differences are great when comparing European, African, and Asian cultures—different languages, different dress, different family structures, different schedules. There are lesser but significant cultural differences between rural villages, suburban towns, and city neighborhoods.

Church life across America is filled with these cultural varieties. The Northeast is more Roman Catholic, while the South is more Baptist and Methodist, and where I live in Minnesota, we have lots of Lutherans. Even if you aren't connected to dominant cultural groups, your area is likely shaped by them. Consider the impact of time zones on the culture of the church. On the East Coast and the West Coast, television shows begin an hour later than in the Midwest. Most local evening news programs begin at 10:00 p.m. in the Midwest and at 11:00 p.m. on the East Coast and on the West Coast. This leads many people on the coasts to go to bed later at night and sleep later in the morning. Churches have adapted to the differences with activities starting earlier in the Midwest and later on the coasts.

When Wooddale Church planned to launch a Saturday evening church service, we conducted a careful survey of all the churches in the Twin Cities area that also had Saturday services. Virtually all of them were

Catholic churches, and they had services that began at 5:00 or 5:15 p.m. We felt that this was too early for summer services in a northern state like ours, where there can be sunlight as late as 10:00 p.m. So we decided to start the service at 6:00 p.m. instead. We found that it didn't work. Perhaps it was because people wanted to go out for dinner after the service and the restaurants were all packed by 7:00 p.m. Or maybe it was because the service attracted realtors, flight attendants, and others who had to get up early for work on Sunday and wanted to come home earlier after the Saturday service. Or perhaps it just didn't fit with our culture, a culture where Catholic churches had long ago set the "right time" for a Saturday service at around 5:00 p.m. We got the cultural message and switched to a 5:15 p.m. start time and found that it worked much better.

Smart church leaders are constantly studying the local culture and adapting to it as necessary. If you are a leader who was born and raised in the area where you now live and attend church, then you probably have an intuitive sense of cultural norms and how they affect volunteers. If you grew up somewhere else, you probably have to look, listen, and ask to learn the local culture. Be sure you are adjusting to the cultural patterns of your fellow volunteers.

Remember That God Is in the Details

"God is in the details" was a frequent claim attributed to the German American architect Ludwig Mies van der Rohe (1886–1969). As an architect, van der Rohe knew that details matter. If you place a wall in the wrong place or don't begin with a level foundation, your building will have problems. Details are important for architecture, and details are important for volunteers.

The church of Jesus Christ is a volunteer church. God has a grand vision for Christ's church, but God is in the details as well. He is present when you are discussing the best time to set for a meeting, when you are trying to figure out child care, and when you are selecting the right curriculum for a second-grade Sunday school class. He is in the details of setting budgets, and he cares about the snacks you choose for vacation Bible school. Much of the work volunteers do day after day, week after week, year after year is about the details. They are essential for the church to be the church.

~~~~~~~~~~~~

Make Prayer a Priority

LEITH

One of the most memorable church board meetings I had as the senior pastor of Wooddale Church was the evening when the chairman handed three pieces of paper to each board member. The first piece was 8½ × 11 inches with three punch holes, the second piece was 5½ × 8½ inches with three punch holes, and the third piece was the size of a credit card with no punch holes. All three had the same information printed on them — the names of all the board members along with the names of all of their family members (spouses and children).

The chairman passed out the three items to each of us and told us that we could choose whichever size worked best for us — the large notebook size, the small notebook size, or the wallet size. Then he said that he was vowing before God and the board as witnesses that he would pray for everyone on the list every day. He didn't just announce it to our group of ten. He looked at each one of us, spoke our name, and said, "I promise I will pray for you, your wife, and your children every day. I will not miss one day. I will pray for you and yours 365 days of the year." Then he invited every board member to make the same commitment. Each one of us spoke the words, one at a time, to each of our fellow board volunteers, making the same promises. It was a powerful spiritual experience, never to be forgotten.

Let there be no doubt that this level of praying for one another is unifying, empowering, and transforming. There were no arguments or divisiveness in our succeeding board meetings. Absenteeism was close to zero. You can't help but love those who pray for you, your spouse, and your children every day.

But there is more to this than a commitment to mutually support one another. When you pray daily for others, you put God at the center of what you do, whether serving on the church board, organizing a short-term missions trip, raising money for a new building, or mentoring teenagers. Prayer is a powerful declaration that the church is not about the pastor, the program, or your personal preferences. You volunteer in the church of Jesus Christ. You serve Jesus, and Jesus is at the center of his church.

Starting at the Top

There is a fascinating story reported in Acts 6 about the priorities of the early church. Good Friday, Easter, the ascension of Jesus, and Pentecost were all past, and the church was now getting established. Almost immediately there was a problem, because problems are a normal part of organizations and relationships between people. The problem was that some widows didn't think they were being fairly treated. To further complicate the conflict, there was an undercurrent of ethnic prejudice bubbling to the surface.

The Jerusalem church was growing, and that was good. But the complaints and problems threatened that growth. And they threatened the unity of the church.

"In those days when the number of disciples was increasing, the Grecian Jews among them complained against the Hebraic Jews because their widows were being overlooked in the daily distribution of food. So the Twelve gathered all the disciples together and said, 'It would not be right for us to neglect the ministry of the word of God in order to wait on tables. Brothers, choose seven men from among you who are known to be full of the Spirit and wisdom. We will turn this responsibility over to them and will give our attention to prayer and the ministry of the word.'"

"This proposal pleased the whole group. They chose Stephen, a man full of faith and of the Holy Spirit; also Philip, Procorus, Nicanor, Timon, Parmenas, and Nicolas from Antioch, a convert to Judaism.

They presented these men to the apostles, who prayed and laid their hands on them" (Acts 6:1–6).

The leaders gathered to discuss the problem. As they formulated a solution, they had to decide the priority of leadership. Should the apostles focus on better management of finances or on resolving cultural differences? Should they spend time trying to grow their numbers? After talking, the group decided that prayer was their priority: "We will turn this responsibility over to them and will give our attention to prayer and the ministry of the word."

This is a case study in masterful management. The leaders of the early church recognized the problem they faced and dealt with it quickly. Everyone was treated with honor and respect. Capable volunteers were recruited, and the finances were delegated to them. All seven of the money-management volunteers had Greek names; this meant that they were sympathetic to the complaints of Grecian widows, and the Grecian widows could trust the men who were chosen. The Holy Spirit led the church out of a problem and into a very positive solution.

What's revealing about this is that the top priority for the leaders of the church was prayer. "We will turn this responsibility over to them and will give our attention to prayer and the ministry of the word." Not only was prayer a leadership priority; it was their public practice: the apostles "prayed and laid their hands on them." And what happened in the church when prayer was the top priority? "So the word of God spread. The number of disciples in Jerusalem increased rapidly, and a large number of priests became obedient to the faith" (Acts 6:7).

This is a prototype for every church. Not every church will face the same issues, but every church will face relational conflicts and disagreements. First-century church leaders put prayer ahead of all other concerns, and they were aggressive and wise in addressing the concerns and needs of people in the church. They publicly prayed over the volunteers they recruited so they would have God's blessing, the support of leadership, and recognition in front of fellow believers.

Pray Continuously

We all know that prayer is important. Centuries ago some very diligent Christians tried to actually "pray continually," as we are instructed in

1 Thessalonians 5:17. Living in monasteries or otherwise isolated from usual community life, they attempted to keep their prayers flowing all day every day. They even tried to keep their mouths moving while they were sleeping so that their continual prayers were truly continual.

While they meant well, the reality is that we do not need to retreat to a monastery to keep prayer a priority in our lives. Most of us have to eat, work, and go to the dentist, and continual vocalized prayers are hard to do in these situations. Besides, nonstop praying probably isn't what the apostle Paul had in mind. The idea is more like having a chronic cough. If you cough continually, it means that your life is regularly punctuated by coughs, but that you also talk, write, think, and sleep between coughs. That's what continuous prayer is like—all of life is punctuated by prayers, even when we wake up in the middle of the night.

And of course there is more to pray about than the work we do as volunteers in the church. We also have family relationships, medical concerns, financial challenges, and neighbors we would like to see come to have a personal relationship with Jesus Christ. We can pray for simple things like a good parking place when we are late for a meeting. Continuous praying connects us to God in all aspects of our lives and reminds us that God is in the details. It reminds us that all of life matters to God and that he is intimately involved in our lives. As volunteers and as leaders of volunteers, prayer for others and their ministries should be an important regular *part* of our prayers.

Focused Prayers

Since we can't pray all the time for everyone, we need to focus our prayers. Those on the Wooddale Church board focused on their fellow board members and their families. There may have been other people on their prayer lists throughout the year, but these people were a primary focus.

In my own prayer life, I have developed a two-pronged approach that helps me stay focused in my prayers. The first prong is a chart with lists of people to pray for each day of the week. There is a list of extended family members divided into seven parts so that everyone in my extended family is prayed for at least once each week. There is also a list of neighbors, spread over seven days. And there is a list of volunteers with whom I am most connected, again divided into seven days with some for every day. This first prong has a Monday group of people to pray for that includes family, neighbors, volunteers, coworkers, and others. There is a similar list for all the other days of every week.

The second prong of my prayer focus is a monthly prayer list for every day. I write up a new list on the last day of every month and then pray through that list each morning, checking off the date every day at the top of the list. This list includes worship of God, personal and immediate family matters, decisions that are pending, coming commitments, health needs of neighbors and friends, and a short list of colleagues and volunteers with significant current opportunities or challenges. Sometimes the same person is on both lists. On Tuesdays I may pray for her because she is leading a neighborhood Bible study, but every day I pray for her because she is receiving chemotherapy. The list changes through the month, sometimes with additions and sometimes with a mark that the prayer has been answered.

When Paul wrote to the church of Thessalonica, he challenged them to pray continually and reported that he prayed for them: "Night and day we pray most earnestly that we may see you again and supply what is lacking in your faith" (1 Thess. 3:10). But he also asked them to pray for him and his fellow volunteers: "Brothers, pray for us" (1 Thess. 5:25).

Prayer declares dependence on God and engagement of God in the lives and work of volunteers. Volunteering is a lot easier when God is the center of our focus—yes, number one on the team. Plus, it is indescribably encouraging to know that others care enough to pray for you regularly.

Should everyone in every church pray for all of the volunteers in that church? No, that's probably not practical. Instead, the leaders in the church can set an example of focused prayer for chosen volunteers and encourage others in the church to also have a cadre of volunteers for whom they regularly pray. The goal is to have so many in the church praying for one another that the congregation becomes a matrix of overlapping circles of prayer. Everyone doesn't pray for everyone, but everyone prays for *someone*. Everyone doesn't pray for everyone, but everyone is prayed for by somebody. When the circles are overlapping, it means that most volunteers have at least two and maybe more fellow believers praying for them. Most of the circles and most of the prayers are typically among those who volunteer in teams or who are directly benefitted by the volunteers for whom they pray.

Involve the Entire Church

Getting the whole church to pray for volunteers is wonderful, but hard to accomplish. The large majority of Christians pray every day, but most of those prayers are about personal, family, and local needs, not about church programs and volunteers.

What can church leaders do to get everyone praying for those who serve? One less than successful approach is to motivate people with guilt. Please don't preach a sermon, write a blog, or give a speech trying to shame people into praying. Sometimes motivation by guilt comes via reports of great prayer warriors who have spent long hours every day praying for others. Sometimes it appears in stories from other countries where Christians arise at 4:00 a.m. to attend daily church prayer gatherings. Thank God for those who so faithfully and sacrificially pray for others, but don't expect a sermon or a blog to convince very many to do the same.

Most Christians want to pray more but really don't know how. They are like the sincere businessman who took a day off work to pray, got down on his knees at sunrise, and prayed about everything and for everyone he could think of. He found he was finished fifteen minutes later. We can all use help in learning how to pray more and how to pray better.

A good place to start is an all-church annual prayer list. Limit this list to four items. An example might look like this:

1. God—that he will be honored in everything at our church

2. Africa—that the millions of new Christians will become fully devoted followers of Jesus

3. Volunteers—that God will encourage all our church volunteers and grow their number by 20 percent in the coming year

4. Cancer—that researchers will make major progress in diagnosing, treating, and curing cancer in our nation

That's not what *you* would put in a four-item list? Okay, what would you suggest? You are well on your way to creating an all-church annual prayer list for the coming year.

Change your list every year. Make posters. Print the list for everyone in the church to have a copy. Make four times more copies of the list than there are people in the church so they can be redistributed through the year and lost copies can easily be replaced. Include the list in church publications, announcements, and public prayers. All this will give congregants specific topics for prayer, including volunteers.

Regularly communicate the names and ministries of volunteers in the congregation. It's great for this to happen on an annual volunteer-recognition Sunday, but even better to have a weekly or monthly list. If the church is large, it may take fifty-two weekly lists to cover everyone. If the church is small, there can be repeats throughout the year that reinforce the value of volunteers and increase their prayer support.

What if volunteers don't want their names published or want to keep a particular ministry private? Someone volunteering at a rape crisis center may be most effective by insisting on confidentiality. Yet these volunteers still need and want prayer support. One solution is to recruit a team of people to pray just for this ministry and these volunteers. To gain the prayers of the whole church, use initials or pseudonyms rather than the volunteers' actual names. Give a substitute name or a broad description of the ministry instead of the actual name of the organization.

Invite the whole congregation to pray for volunteers silently in some church services in different months. If the printed list is long, ask people to pray "right now" for

1. two of the people you know;

2. two of the people you don't know;

3. the names starting with the same letter as your last name;

4. those volunteering in areas where you have a particular interest or burden, maybe where you would like to volunteer yourself.

The main point is to get the church praying for volunteers, using creative suggestions and multiple opportunities.

Pray for Needs

Churches that care about people usually have more volunteer opportunities than people signing up. No one wants to announce that "we don't have a Sunday school teacher for third-grade boys, and we're either going to have to close the class or combine them with first and second graders unless someone volunteers by noon on Friday. Please pray that someone will answer the call of God and step up to teach these boys." This approach seldom produces the best teacher for third graders, but the need is real, and what else can be done?

Invite the entire congregation to pray for the best volunteers for specific ministries. If the prayer is for a third-grade teacher, start the praying in April, not in August, when school is getting ready to start. Present the prayer request as an opportunity rather than a problem.

Think about setting up prayer teams of people who will commit to pray specifically for volunteer needs for a limited period of time, like three or six months. Ask four church members if they will join the team to hear about the most pressing needs of the church and commit to pray daily for God's direction and provision. Tell them that after three months of intensive prayer, they will be replaced by a new team.

Prayer involves listening and not just asking. At one time during my pastorate, I was burdened by the church's lack of ministry to persons with special developmental needs and their families. I prayed. I asked others to pray. I attempted to recruit volunteers to set up a ministry. Months passed into years with no volunteers and no new special-needs ministry. After a long time and a lot of prayers, it suddenly came together. There were multiple volunteers, some with extensive experience. This ministry began well and flourished. God was asked. God blessed with waiting. Prayers continued. God provided.

Praying for God to meet needs doesn't require waiting for a crisis. Plan ahead. Invite everyone in the congregation to pray for God's vision for the church in the year ahead. Have them write down suggestions for programs, ministries, finances, and staff. Encourage them to think beyond the church and into the community and around the world. The church board or a task force can review all the good suggestions and recommend three or four to become the prayer focus in the near future.

As leaders, we are well aware of the responsibility of stewarding our volunteers. But just as important, if not more important, is that of shepherding—coming alongside, walking with, and caring for those who partner with us in ministry.

Brian was a volunteer in our junior-high ministry. An accountant by profession, his eye for detail and accountability served us well as we organized a group of three hundred middle-graders. Three of my monthly meetings with him stand out. First was the day he gave me a tour of his new window-with-a-view office after becoming a partner in the firm. We celebrated together over lunch in the executive dining room, planning how the company's hockey season tickets might possibly create a memorable outing for the students. Nine months later he came to my office to share the news he'd been let go in a restructuring. He was devastated and dreaded having to tell his wife. We wept together, read Scripture (Psalm 46 in particular), and prayed. God was there with us that day, and as Brian left, he said, "I can't wait to see what God is going to do with this one!" Three months later at a local diner he told me he was starting a new job that he described as "my dream job!"

I was reminded that day and many since of the importance of shepherding. One of the ways we can be that shepherd to volunteers is by coming alongside, being present, walking with them, and caring in practical ways.

—Ken

Then the whole church can start praying for enough volunteers to staff the Sunday school, launch a ministry for persons with special needs, help build a home for a poor family, go on an evangelistic outreach in another state or nation, send a college student to seminary, support a needy child in a developing nation, or whatever other exciting opportunity God provides.

Prayer Is a Win-Win

Godly people want their church to be a praying church but aren't sure how to make that happen. Churches want lots of volunteers but don't know where to get them. Prayer can be the answer to both. We have people who want to volunteer but are trying to figure out how. We have ministries that need volunteers but are trying to figure out who. We have unseen opportunities to serve God and others but are trying to figure out what they are. The way to link all these together is prayer.

Prayer is a win-win. The more people learn to pray, the more they like to pray. The more answers to prayer, the more prayers are prayed. Volunteers and volunteer opportunities are easy to understand and easy to pray about. The outcome is a praying church, effective volunteers, and serving others in the name of Jesus from the church nursery to the far corners of the globe.

Volunteer Development Training

GROWING GREATNESS

A Training Plan for Staff and Those Who Lead Volunteers

It's not about giving your time;
it's about expanding your life.
Be a part of what God is doing.

Why

What is volunteer development?

Volunteer development is a church's effort to train, support, and encourage ministry leaders as they recruit and nurture lay leaders and volunteers. It also seeks to help staff and volunteer leaders work more effectively with their volunteers.

Why is it important?

Many church ministries are volunteer-driven, and, whenever possible, recruiting gifted volunteers rather than increasing staff is going to be more effective in the life of the church.

Why a volunteer development program?

• Through volunteering, people in and beyond the church come to faith in Jesus Christ.

- Volunteers have an enormous impact on a church's ability to provide opportunities to members, attendees, and visitors.
- Volunteering is one of the best ways for people to connect and make friends.
- Volunteering is a form of worship.
- Volunteering gives a congregation opportunities to have an impact, grow the kingdom of God, and be involved in something big even when the effort might appear to be small.
- Volunteering is transforming; it changes the volunteers' lives, changes the lives of those they serve, and helps everyone involved grow as disciples of Jesus Christ.

What are the goals of volunteer development training?

- Engage more of the local church in the faith-building activity of volunteering.
- Reward volunteers and increase their satisfaction.
- Increase the longevity of volunteers' service.
- Assist leaders in attracting greater numbers of volunteers.
- Help resolve frustrations (of both leaders and volunteers).
- Build effective volunteer teams.
- Impact God's kingdom.

Prayer

Thank God for your volunteers. Pray for God's wisdom and direction as you move forward with volunteer development in your ministry.

How

Volunteer development has five key steps:

1. Recruit
2. Train
3. Build the team
4. Appreciate and Celebrate
5. Empower

STEP 1: RECRUIT

Occasionally recruitment is passive (a wonderful church member hears about a particular ministry and wants to get involved). Sometimes broadcasting an open volunteer position through a church newsletter or through other public means can yield a volunteer. But most often recruitment requires that an individual be asked to join the ministry. How can the likelihood of a potential volunteer jumping in be increased?

To effectively recruit, a role description for every volunteer position must be prepared so expectations are clear from the outset. Each description should include:

- Title—a straightforward "handle" such as *teacher's assistant* that is clear to everyone
- Purpose—why is this role important?
- Description—a simple, one-sentence explanation of the role
- Responsibilities—a list of requirements and tasks
- Qualifications—experience, skills, interests

Where do you find prospective volunteers?

- Commission current volunteers to identify prospective volunteers.
- Network with people you know.
- Ask staff whether they know someone who might qualify.
- Church newsletter, webpage, social networking

How do you connect with a prospective volunteer?

- Identify your potential volunteer—strengths, interests, and spiritual gifts. Know what other ministries he or she might be involved in.
- Consider particular ways of making contact—in person, via a letter, email, phone call, or over coffee. Which method will be most effective with the person you are trying to reach?
- Introduce yourself and make a personal connection. Do you know this individual or someone else who does? What do you share in common?
- Share with the potential volunteers why you thought of them, who recommended them, and why.

- Invite the potential volunteer to participate in what God is doing in your ministry area. Mention the exciting things that have been accomplished and will be occurring in the weeks and months ahead.
- Be specific about the role you had in mind (use the role descriptions you created) and state the time commitment up front.
- Follow up in a timely fashion with a call, postcard, or email.
- Stay in touch. If you get a "no for now," find ways to inform your prospective volunteer of what's going on in that ministry or other ministries. Keep the invitation open.
- Have faith. Pray about your recruiting efforts and for potential volunteers.

Talk

- Is it easy or difficult to recruit volunteers to your ministry area?

_____

_____

_____

_____

_____

- What are some ways you can better recruit volunteers in your ministry?

_____

_____

_____

_____

_____

Ideas

- Teach your volunteers to always be looking for potential volunteers.
- Celebrate when someone asks a new individual to be a part of the team.
- Keep your ministry's social media areas updated.
- Refer potential volunteers to the best place in your church building for finding out about ministry opportunities.
- Set an appropriate time frame with your team for following up with volunteers.

- Delegate a specific person to be responsible for contacting and following up with prospective volunteers.
- Think of creative ways you can use social networking.
- Remain positive even when recruiting is frustrating.
- Keep the door open for a different opportunity if a potential recruit is reluctant.

STEP 2: TRAIN

All new volunteers deserve to have effective training so they are set up to succeed in their new role.

- Use role descriptions for the training of each new volunteer.
- Ask new volunteers what they hope to get out of the volunteer role so you can help them develop and succeed.
- Discuss your volunteers' goals and desires for the ministry and for the volunteer team.
- Have an experienced volunteer available to mentor and answer questions for each new volunteer until he or she is comfortable with the role.
- Give each new volunteer a tour of your area, showing where things are and introducing him or her to the team.

Talk

- How do you presently train your volunteers?

_____

_____

_____

_____

- How can you enhance your training to be more consistent and effective?

_____

_____

_____

_____

_____

Ideas

- As you go through the training, talk with your team leaders about what unique ideas they can add to their ministry. ("I will send one thank-you note per month to each of my volunteers.")
- Additional training may be needed that is specific to your ministry area in order for your volunteers to succeed.
- Train volunteer leaders to recruit more volunteers.
- Check in periodically with your volunteers to see if additional training, encouragement, or support are needed.

STEP 3: BUILD THE TEAM

- Make your ministry area a place where new people feel loved and welcome. Help your volunteers to get to know the new person on the team and overwhelm new volunteers with friendship and appreciation. (If you've ever walked into a party where everybody else knows each other and you're the odd one out, you know how uncomfortable it feels to be the outsider. Don't let this happen in your ministry!)
- Share successes. Develop a system of communicating experiences—not just grand achievements but also individual stories. Success is about more than programs; it's about people. How can stories ricochet through your ministry and encourage your volunteers to understand the impact their team is making?
- Pray for each other. Develop an informal email list that people can use to keep in contact and share prayer concerns not just about ministry-related issues but also about personal concerns and praises.
- As you train, look for what the individual is expecting to attain out of this role and ask yourself whether he or she is a potential leader. Can this person be a team leader or be more effective in another role? Paying attention to these details will help you form effective teams.
- Check in often with your volunteers for feedback.
- Start meetings on time. Have an agenda and follow it. Always take time for personal prayer requests and sharing. End on time.
- Remember, volunteering is about outreach. The more people you have on your team, the more lives will be impacted for the kingdom.

- Make sure your team members know you care about their ideas, thoughts, and opinions. Use any that you can, and acknowledge where the suggestion came from.
- Get to know your volunteers. Make sure you spend time with them so you know who they are, who their families are, and what makes them tick.

Talk

- How are your team dynamics?

_____

_____

_____

_____

- Is it easy for new people to join your team? Do they feel welcome?

_____

_____

_____

_____

- Do you provide opportunities for your team to give feedback?

_____

_____

_____

_____

Ideas

- Look for ways to grow as a group in community.
- Pray together as a team.
- Send a weekly email asking for prayer requests that can be distributed to the group.
- Have fun together.
- Host a party.
- Serve together in another area or a community outreach project.

- Begin with an occasional icebreaker at team meetings.
- When there is a new team member, send out a welcoming email with fun and interesting facts about him or her.

STEP 4: APPRECIATE AND CELEBRATE

- Celebrate what volunteers are accomplishing as they give their time and grow. Regular support can mean the difference between a volunteer sticking with the ministry or dropping out.
- Be your volunteers' biggest cheerleader, and remember that your words of encouragement matter. Say thank you and write personal notes. Acknowledge what they are doing well.
- The gift of your time is important. Don't be too busy to spend time with each of your volunteers. Check in regularly during your volunteers' time of service, even with very dependable and committed volunteers, so they don't feel abandoned or taken for granted.
- Pray for and with your volunteers.

Talk

- When was the last time you thanked your volunteers and wrote them a thank-you letter?

_____

_____

_____

_____

_____

- How often do you check in with your volunteers to see whether they are enjoying their volunteer experience?

_____

_____

_____

_____

_____

Ideas

- Thank volunteers.
- Always pass along compliments.
- Be wary of bringing up a negative issue unless it must be shared in order to correct a problem.
- Send a note or email.
- Give a call.
- Listen.
- Go for coffee.
- Have a party to celebrate all you have achieved together.

STEP 5: EMPOWER

- Give lay leaders the empowerment they need in order to do a good job. Train them thoroughly and give them permission to pursue goals with your help.
- Help paint a vision of what could be accomplished by this team. What are they a part of? Let them know you're in the work together.
- Be sensitive to burnout. Give lay leaders permission to contact you with issues or concerns. Propose ways that problems can be solved or responsibilities rotated. Find ways to refresh volunteers.
- Accept that a current role may not be forever. If an individual is looking for a new ministry role inside or outside of the church, be supportive. If appropriate, help him or her to find a new place to serve.
- Remember to delegate responsibilities to team members. It is an opportunity for them to grow as potential leaders.

Talk

- Do you allow your leaders to lead? How good are you at delegating?

_____

_____

_____

_____

- How do you respond when a volunteer resigns?

_____

_____

_____

_____

Ideas

- Help your volunteers discover their potential. Encourage them to take a spiritual gifts test or another assessment tool. Refer them to a class on spiritual gifts.
- Let your lay leaders lead, but be consistently supportive and available to them.
- Find a leadership conference you can take them to.
- Recommend a book to read together as a team to help your volunteers grow.

Q & A

- Do you have questions or issues that you'd like to discuss?

_____

_____

_____

_____

Prayer

Ask God to make you sensitive to the needs of volunteers so you can be a good steward of their gifts of time and talents. Ask God to provide new ways to use volunteers' gifts.

Your Plan for Volunteer Development

Volunteer development is about more than getting additional volunteers. It's about changing your ministry, your church, the volunteers themselves, and expanding the kingdom through the efforts of ordinary people.

Your Vision

- What is God's vision for your ministry? How will you use volunteers to accomplish God's vision?

_____

_____

_____

_____

_____

Your Plan

- What goals do you have for volunteer development in the coming year? How will you achieve these goals?

_____

_____

_____

_____

_____

_____

_____

_____

Your Team

STEP 1: RECRUIT

- Who will be responsible for communicating to *all* volunteers the importance of inviting others to join the volunteer team?

_____

_____

_____

_____

_____

- Who will keep your area of the website updated? Who will be responsible for updating the volunteer opportunities webpage?

_____

_____

_____

_____

_____

- Who will be responsible for writing up volunteer successes for the church to share and celebrate?

_____

_____

_____

_____

_____

- Other thoughts on recruiting?

_____

_____

_____

_____

_____

STEP 2: TRAIN

- Who will create the role descriptions? When will they be complete?

_____
_____
_____
_____
_____

- Who will make sure all lay leaders are trained?

_____
_____
_____
_____

- Who will you delegate to be with new team members until they are comfortable with their new roles?

_____
_____
_____
_____
_____

- Other thoughts on training?

_____
_____
_____
_____

STEP 3: BUILD THE TEAM

- Who will be responsible for communicating ministry success stories? What are the vehicles in your church for getting the word out?

_____

_____

_____

_____

_____

- Who will be responsible to welcome new team members and introduce them to the rest of the team?

_____

_____

_____

_____

_____

- Who will be responsible for collecting and distributing prayer requests?

_____

_____

_____

_____

_____

- Other thoughts on team building?

_____

_____

_____

_____

_____

STEP 4: APPRECIATE AND CELEBRATE

- Who will plan and coordinate appreciation efforts? (e.g., thank-you notes, parties, etc.)

_____

_____

_____

_____

_____

- Who will develop a system to check in with volunteers while they are serving?

_____

_____

_____

_____

_____

- Other thoughts on appreciation?

_____

_____

_____

_____

STEP 5: EMPOWER

- Which of your volunteers could be leaders or be delegated more responsibilities? What are some ways to make it happen?

_____

_____

_____

_____

_____

- Other thoughts on empowerment?

_____

_____

_____

_____

_____

Q & A

- What questions or issues would you like to discuss?

_____

_____

_____

_____

_____

Prayer

Ask God for his help in implementing a new plan to recruit and nurture volunteers. Thank him for his direction as you move forward.

NOTES

1. Joanna Saisan, M.S.W., Melinda Smith, M.A., and Gina Kemp, M.A., "Volunteering and Its Surprise Benefits," Helpguide: A Trusted Non-Profit Resource, last updated December 2014, *http://www.helpguide.org/life/ volunteer_opportunities_benefits_volunteering.htm.*

2. United States Department of Labor, Bureau of Labor Statistics, "Volunteering in the United States, 2013," news release, February 25, 2014, *http:// www.bls.gov/news.release/volun.nr0.htm.*

3. Ibid.

4. Ibid.

5. "Adopt a Highway," *Wikipedia*, last modified June 5, 2014, *http://en.wikipedia .org/wiki/Adopt_a_Highway.*

6. Sara Wheeler, *Cherry: A Life of Apsley Cherry-Garrard* (New York: Jonathan Cape, 2001), 187.

7. Two books by Leith Anderson will be helpful for developing church leaders: *Leadership That Works* (Minneapolis: Bethany House, 1999) and *Dying for Change* (Minneapolis: Bethany House, 1990).

8. Laurie Blake, "Volunteers Become Vital at City Hall," *Star Tribune*, March 9, 2014, B3.

9. Ibid.

10. Ibid., B5.

11. Leslie B. Flynn, *Nineteen Gifts of the Spirit* (Colorado Springs: Cook, 1994).

12. For a detailed description of how this works in a church, see *Winning on Purpose* by John Edmund Kaiser (Nashville: Abingdon, 2006).

13. *http://en.wikipedia.org/wiki/Eastern_Air_Lines_Flight_401.*